Finding HOPE

Finding HOPE

THE JOURNEY *from* DARK DESPAIR TO LIBERATING LIGHT

RANDY L. BOTT

CFI
An Imprint of Cedar Fort, Inc.
Springville, Utah

ISBN 13: 978-1-4621-3704-6

Published by CFI, an imprint of Cedar Fort, Inc.
2373 W. 700 S., Springville, UT, 84663
Distributed by Cedar Fort, Inc., www.cedarfort.com

Library of Congress Control Number: 2020948513

Cover design by Shawnda T. Craig

Printed in the United States of America

10 9 8 7 6 5 4 3 2 1

Printed on acid-free paper

To those countless people who,
when facing their darkest hour,
turned to the Light.

CONTENTS

ACKNOWLEDGMENT

To my good friend and constant sounding-board, Steve Coltrin. He was the one who gave me the idea and then pushed me to put on paper principles we have discussed over the past four decades. Without his constant encouragement, this work would have never seen the Light of day!

PROLOGUE

The story is told of a father who had two sons. He desperately wanted them to be successful in life, but it seemed their stubbornness and unwillingness to follow any other than their own way of thinking would destine them to less than optimal success. Deciding on a course of action, this wise father concocted a plan.

He called the two sons into his palatial study and explained the rules for the contest. Using only the resources within the study, they were to discover the combination to his safe within a certain time limit. If successful, each boy would win the contents of the safe. The father showed the boys the prizes: deeds to two large pieces of industrial property and two envelopes with a huge amount of cash. Only one deed and one envelope was to be placed in the safe at a time. Each boy could win. They were not competing with each other.

The rules of the contest allowed only one boy into the room at a time. No other person other than the observing father was allowed into the room during the contest. By the toss of a coin it was determined that the elder brother would go first. The hour time limit seemed to be ample for such an easy task.

With the younger son anxiously awaiting his turn in the hallway, the the father escorted the elder son into the study. Commencing at the desk, the elder son rifled through the papers, drawers, and files, looking for the combination to the safe. Minutes ticked away and frustration began to take its toll. Books from the study shelves were removed and examined for the elusive combination. As the hour began to wane, the boy frantically looked under the carpet, in the sofa, inside the lamp shade, and in every other conceivable hiding place. Not infrequently he verbally complained about the impossibility and stupidity of the contest. At last the hour concluded with him frantically trying to "feel" the clicks of the combination as he rotated the dial lock. Dejected and angry, he was escorted from the room. He had failed to win the prize.

The younger son was escorted into the study to the sound of warnings from the elder brother that it was a stupid contest and he may as well quit before he started because he would never find the combination. The search began in much the same manner with the younger son as it had with the elder son. The father stood quietly in the shadows with arms folded, watching the fruitless search of his younger son.

About fifteen minutes into the search it seemed as though a light bulb turned on in the mind of the searching son. He paused, looked at his father, and queried: "Did you say I could use any resource within the room?" The father answered in the affirmative. In an obvious voice of triumphant elation, the younger son asked, "Dad, what is the combination to the safe?" To his relief and joy, his father slowly repeated the combination. The dial on the safe's lock was rotated at the direction of the father, stopping precisely on the designated numbers. Gone was the frustration, the anxiety, and the hurry. Replacing the agitated dismay was a sense of peace and humble willingness to follow directions. As the father ceased speaking, the younger son reached for the handle. As he applied pressure, he felt the latch give, and with considerable effort he pulled open the safe's door to claim his prize.

With an embrace and tears of gratitude, he and his father exited the room to find the elder son still fuming over his defeat. In a voice of total unbelief, the elder son asked how the younger son had succeeded in opening the safe. Still beaming over his success, the younger son explained that he had asked his father for the combination. Now in total exasperation the elder son ranted and raved about the unfairness of the father. Why hadn't the father told him the combination? Without answering, the father turned to the younger son, who explained, "Dad said we could use *all* resources within the study. He was in the study and certainly was a knowledgeable resource, so I asked him. You never did ask!"

Such is the story. The application of the principle is probably self-evident. We are sent into mortality with a difficult task to perform—

negotiate the challenges of life and return to the presence of the Father. We have been promised by the Father that we may use all resources available to complete the task. He is not an absentee God but a loving, concerned, willing Father. He will not perform the task (opening the safe) for us, but He will, if we ask, give us the directions enabling us to open the safe ourselves. Inside the safe is far more than the deed to some real estate and an envelope with a huge sum of money. Inside is a promised reward: "Then shall the King say unto them on his right hand, Come, ye blessed of my Father, **inherit the kingdom** prepared for you from the foundation of the world" (Matthew 25:34, emphasis added).

Many a man and many a woman have exited the contest of mortality in total frustration, with protestation about the impossibility of the task. Others have defiantly raised their clenched fists toward the heavens, claiming favoritism because some have successfully asked the Father for the combination and have received positive confirmation of the promise: "Ask, and it shall be given you; seek, and ye shall find; knock, and it shall be opened unto you: For **every one** that asketh receiveth; and he that seeketh findeth; and to him that knocketh it shall be opened" (Matthew 7:7–8, emphasis added).

What a disappointment to arrive at our final interview with the Father when our mortal lives will be reviewed in detail only to discover that we received from life exactly what we wanted and expected. How singularly beautiful the promise of the Lord: "And in that day ye shall ask me nothing. Verily, verily, I say unto you, Whatsoever ye shall ask the Father in my name, he will give it you" (John 16:23).

While there is still time, I encourage all to draw near to the Lord and receive the divine promise that "I will not leave you comfortless: I will come to you" (John 14:18).

I testify from my own personal experiences that communicating with the Father is not only possible but achievable. The results of His constant answers to humble pleadings brings joy in this life and a lively hope of eternal life in the world to come. Stay focused on the Savior and His Father, and They will tutor you through the challenges of mortality back to Their presence to receive eternal life.

INTRODUCTION

If you live a long time, you will grow old! This seems like a no-brainer statement, but the advantage of a long life is that it provides opportunities to observe, interface with, be influenced by, and possibly influence a variety of people. Some people are very successful, and (unfortunately) many mirror the frustration of the elder son described in the prologue. It isn't that the tests and trials of life are significantly different, although, on the surface, some tests may seem easier than others. It is the approach various individuals take as they embrace the challenges of life or retreat from them.

This book is not intended to answer all of life's challenges. It is definitely not written to condemn or lay a guilt trip on anyone. I will draw upon my seventy-plus years of experience being a participant in life's challenges myself, observing others as they struggle to make sense of the seemingly senseless, learning from the counsel of others, and trying to help those who are willing to accept advice and help to meet their daily challenges.

I will refer to real people and real challenges. For obvious reasons I will not use the real names of those individuals described. Seventy years of experience has provided more examples than can possibly be contained in one book. Deciding which examples to use has been a difficult but necessary choice given the restricted length of the book.

You may not find all of the examples of interest to you. You may see other principles that are not noted but have significance in your own life or the lives of those you love and care about.

Not all stories will be the same length. Some can be told in a few pages; others will require more detail in order to make sense of the people's struggles. I suspect that you, the reader, could compile a number of scenarios of even greater significance.

In writing this book, I do not claim to have mastered all of the principles outlined. But I genuinely hope that you will overlook my weaknesses and see the desire I have to help everyone I meet turn toward the Light and find the peace, direction, and purpose God intends us to have as we sequence through our earthly experience. I disclose at the beginning that I believe that God not only exists but is interested in every individual on earth and is anxiously waiting for us to look to Him for help and direction in coping with the frustrating challenges of life. He is not an absentee God but, like the father in the prologue, is only waiting for us to respond to His invitation to "come unto me" (Matthew 11:28).

In telling each person's story, I will refer to the contrast between darkness and light. Whether or not you believe in the devil and evil, each story illustrates what the individuals described as the difference between the suffocating, ever-darkening blackness they experienced as they turned their collective backs on the Light. Then they will contrast those feelings with the ever-increasing, liberating feelings associated with facing the Light.

Each story will be told in first person with some exceptions where my narrating the experience seems more appropriate. The impact these stories had, and continue to have, on my life has cemented the principles in my mind. If some of the wording is not in perfect character, I take full responsibility for that. Please don't trip over the verbiage and miss the principle. Noting that many of these experiences happened years ago, I will still write, to the best of my memory, the recounting as the participants related them to me.

Now the task lies with you, the reader. You do not have to take the challenges outlined in the book. You have been given agency enabling you to make whatever choices you desire in your quest to find happiness and fulfillment in life. But know assuredly that when you pick up one end of a stick, the other end inescapably follows. Not all consequences are immediate, but they will come. So, being intellectually honest with yourself, you and you alone can determine the course of life you will pursue based on the choices you make. It is impossible in nature and in life to pick up one end of a stick and have something other than the God-ordained consequence ensue.

Following each of the vignettes is a brief "Points to Ponder" section containing some questions you may want to consider in applying the principles found in the vignette. Your conclusions may differ from mine—not a problem. You may agree or disagree with my summary. Again, not a problem. My hope is that each question or invitation will act as a catalyst to inspire deeper contemplations that will broaden your understanding of what is happening to you and what visions are open to your mind about possible options to move forward with your life.

The overarching concept upon which this book is written is that there is hope no matter how far you feel you may have detoured from the path of happiness or the God-ordained path. No one has gone beyond the point of no return. No one has postponed change until it is everlasting too late. Know assuredly that the moment you turn your face toward God, He will immediately respond with whatever help He sees you need to reclaim your life, your purpose, and your happiness.

1

A MARINE'S JOURNEY

From Remorse to Relief

Jim was leaning on the railing at Pearl Harbor looking at the memorial of the USS Arizona *when I met him. It was our first and only encounter, but it permanently impacted me. Jim was in his late sixties or early seventies. He was well built, well groomed, and seemed to be the picture of health. The others in our group were browsing through the shops. Because shopping (affectionately referred to by my wife as "retail therapy") ranks near the bottom of my list of things I like to do, I chose to wander the paths near the harbor.*

I approached Jim and said "hello" in passing. He seemed eager to talk, so I joined him. He had a military pin on his lapel indicating that he was a former Marine. I asked him about the pin. He asked if I had time to listen to his story. Since my wife and her friends are born shoppers, I knew I had some time to kill before they were ready to move to the Punchbowl Cemetery to view the thousands of war causalities buried and memorialized there. This is Jim's story:

I joined the Marines when I was nineteen years old. The draft lottery was in force at that time, and I had a number that ensured that I would be drafted. I chose to enlist in the Marines because I envisioned the glory and the toughness portrayed in their recruiting materials.

Boot camp was brutal. The drill sergeants said they were trying to toughen us up for what we would experience in Nam. At times I thought they were trying to kill us before we were deployed. Many washed out of our program and were reassigned to positions of lesser demand. I knew I was as tough as the toughest and no foul-mouthed, foul-breathed, illiterate drill sergeant could break me.

Finally, boot camp was over. I had to admit they had toughened us up and we were in better physical shape than I had ever been in my life. Then came the deployment. We were ready to conquer the world and end the war. The flight to Nam was long and uncomfortable, but that was nothing to a group of battle-ready, hardened leather necks!

Then the reality hit. Nam was hot and humid. Bugs were crawling on us day and night. Even the nights were swelteringly hot. The food was tolerable unless we were on extended patrols—which seemed to be most of the time. The guys in my platoon were from all backgrounds. Some were crude and unable to speak two words without a curse or profanity mixed in. Others were quiet and didn't say much. A few were what I would classify as "normal."

Over the course of months, we adjusted to the environment. The patrols were the most dangerous part of our duties. The Viet Cong would hide in trees, in the dense foliage, in fox holes—anywhere they could not be detected. On more than one occasion we had been ambushed. It was a sorry, sobering day when my best buddy, who was the patrol leader, took a bullet to the head. It killed him instantly. I was appointed patrol leader in his place. From that point on I seemed to be on a revenge mission. I would kill, with some satisfaction, every enemy soldier who came within my sights.

That was all well and good until the day we were assigned to take a small hamlet. We had heard that the Cong would use human shields as they tried to make their escape. Women, men, children, anyone they could find were held between them and us. I hadn't personally seen that scenario, but others told us how difficult it was to have to kill the hostage to get to the enemy soldier. Others told us how the Cong would strap a grenade or bomb to a little child and send her to greet the American soldiers only to blow her and the soldiers up when she got to them. I guess I didn't believe anyone could drop that low or have that little regard for human life.

Then it happened to us. As I mentioned, I was the patrol leader. The rest of the guys followed closely behind as we closed in on the little hamlet. I saw the little girl running toward us holding out her arms as though waiting for an embrace. I noted the bomb strapped to her waist. What was I to do? If I didn't stop her, the Cong would detonate the bomb when she got near us and destroy her and kill or injure many of my patrol. There wasn't a lot of time to make the decision. With more trembling than I had ever known, I raised my rifle, pointed it at the little girl, and fired. The explosion of the bomb annihilated her. She literally disappeared before our eyes. Body parts were blown in all directions. My heart died within me that very instant. What had I done? Did I make the right decision? With what I thought was justifiable vengeance, we leveled the whole hamlet.

The rest of the time in Nam was more like a daze. It seemed like every time I closed my eyes I could see the face of that little girl. Every time a bomb or grenade went off my mind recreated the vision of that little girl evaporating before our eyes. Thankfully our tour soon came to an end. We returned home, and I was discharged from the Marines.

I don't know much about PTSD, except I know it is real and I had a huge case of it. I went from anger to depression and back again so many times I can't begin to count. The more I thought about the killing, the little girl, and the whole senselessness of the war, the more despondent I became. It seemed like a dark cloud was hanging over my head. I couldn't sleep, I had no appetite, no activities held any interest for me, and I couldn't bring myself to try to establish any meaningful relationships. I felt like I was being engulfed in a dark prison with no means of escape.

I hadn't grown up in a religious family, so I didn't think much about God or life having a special purpose. It seemed that everything I had experienced to that point confirmed that life was just a meaningless venture that all people endured until they died, and then that was the end of it. I read accounts of other servicemen who experienced similar feelings and ended up taking their own lives. Somehow, I felt that suicide wasn't a good solution for my problems. Surely there must be a way to break out of that suffocating prison. Life used to be so carefree and happy. Now it was an almost impossible chore to just get up in the morning and put one foot in front of the other. Something had to give. There was no way I could continue like that.

One Sunday I was driving down the street near my home and passed a church house. The services had just concluded, and throngs of people were exiting the building. I noted that they were all smiling, happy, talking, and seemingly enjoying each other's company. What did they know that I didn't? For the first time in my life I decided to try to find out if there really is a God and what my relationship was to Him.

I didn't know how to pray since I don't remember praying before. I am sure my first attempts to pray must have caused God to bust a gut laughing. Although it wasn't smooth and grammatically correct, it certainly was heartfelt as I reached out to whatever is called God and asked for help rescuing me from my prison. I didn't see a vision or hear a voice, but I experienced a feeling that penetrated my very soul. It was like someone had given me an injection of hope. I was so thrilled I didn't know how to act. I wanted to jump and laugh and sing (and I ain't no singer!). When my feet finally hit the ground, I didn't know where to go from there.

Because I knew that church-going people read the Bible, I went to the local bookstore and purchased a Bible. I started reading in Genesis. It was a cool story, but I didn't see how it applied to me. Soon I decided to leaf through the rest of the Bible. I came to Matthew in the New Testament. As I read about Jesus and His teachings, something inside happened. That same euphoria I had experienced when I first prayed came again. I couldn't get enough. I read the four gospels and then the rest of the New Testament. Some of it was hard to understand, but a lot of it gave powerful directions that I could apply to my life.

Almost without realizing it, I came to know that this wasn't just some fable that some ancient people had written. It was really true. Jesus portrayed God as a real person who knew and was interested in people on earth. He actually referred to God as "Our Father." Jesus taught that God is so personal and involved in each person's life that even the very hairs of his head are numbered. That thought blew me away. He talked about how God knew even when a sparrow fell to the ground and then said that each person was of more worth than many sparrows and received more divine attention.

When I grasped the thought of a personal God who knew me, knew my challenges, and invited me to "come unto me all ye that labor and are heavy laden" (Matthew 11:28) with the promise that He would give me rest, I decided to give it a try. It didn't happen all at once, but over time I realized that my enjoyment of life was increasing, I regained my appetite, and my whole countenance brightened. I had a new enthusiasm for life, and that horrible prison that had nearly annihilated me was destroyed. I found that I could develop meaningful relationships with others. I now have a wife, four kids, and eight grandkids, all of whom I dearly love.

I still think occasionally of the little girl in Nam, but now I am actually thankful for what happened. I am not sure where I would be if that hadn't occurred. I have found when I think about that experience, although I don't understand it all, I know that God knows that little girl as well as He knows me and will make everything okay for both of us.

Do I still have challenges in my life? You'd better believe it. But with what has transpired in my life, I am enjoying the sunsets more than the storms. I have lost my fear of the challenges of life. I know if I keep facing God and trying to follow His outlined course that everything will turn out all right."

I almost hated to see our group come looking for me. I thanked Jim for sharing his story with me and wished him the best. We shook hands and he resumed his posture of leaning on the rail looking out toward the USS Arizona. *I have never seen him again, but the vision he created in my mind of his journey from his darkened prison to the light has never left me.*

POINTS TO PONDER

- What would you do if faced with a situation that put two or more of your foundational beliefs in direct opposition?
- Have you ever second-guessed a decision or action you have taken?
- How have you resolved that inner conflict and achieved a peaceful resolution?
- Are there things you could do that would result in even greater peace and contentment?
- Have you experienced that infusion of hope in your own life or witnessed it in the lives of others?

2

DEFEATING GOLIATH

From Addiction to Affirmation

"I'd fight to the death for the right to control my own life," Ken said. I have known Ken for most of his life. He was a normal teenager with all the excesses of energy and hormones. He was raised in a loving, tight-knit family. He had good friends and seemed to be on the path to a successful life. Somewhere along the line his friends introduced him to pornography. At first it was just a curiosity experience. Of course, all young men seemed to be interested in a girl's developing body. However, before long, like an invisible magnet, Ken found himself drawn to view more and more adult sites on the Internet. He recounts:

At first I thought viewing porn was an innocent pastime. All the guys were doing it. We laughed and talked about it. I knew I could stop anytime I wanted to. Almost without my being aware, the sites that had previously created such a sexual rush no longer had the same impact. I started to look at harder and grosser scenes. However, with the passage of time, even the hard porn didn't satisfy my desire to look. Fanaticizing sexual activity replaced reality.

I engaged in the habit—no call it what it was—the addiction. It wasn't until I was about twenty-four that I realized I needed to make a change or porn would ruin my life. How could I marry and expect my wife to participate in the gross sexual scenes I had been viewing for years? So, I decided to go "cold turkey" and quit all together. It was then I realized what a prison cell I had confined myself to. In spite of my strongest promise to myself, I found I would weaken and fall back into watching—promising myself each time that this was the last time I would watch. However, it never was the last time. I rationalized that it really wasn't hurting anyone but myself although I knew that was a lie.

I had always considered myself an intelligent person having a reasoning mind. One day I decided I needed to have a heart-to-heart with myself. I reasoned that I knew that God had created mankind. Therefore, He must have programmed the sexual feelings in His sons and daughters. Therefore, those sexual feelings couldn't be all bad. However, using them in ways that God had specifically forbidden in scriptures must be the source of the negative feelings associated with violating the laws of chastity.

If God had programmed the feelings in mankind, He must also know how to help overcome those who had fallen into the trap of addiction. Having read the Bible as a family for years, I was somewhat familiar with some ideas that might help me. First was the Lord's invitation to "come unto me all ye that labor and are heaven laden"—that was me! He promised, "I will give you rest"—exactly what I was looking for (Matthew 11:28).

I remember the parable of the guy who cast out the evil spirit, and then swept and garnished his house. When the evil spirit returned (just like my relapsing), he found the house clean and empty. He went out and got seven other evil spirits to join him (see Luke 11:24–26). The parable notes that the end was worse than the beginning. That is what I was experiencing with the ever-deepening dive into harder and grosser porn.

So, how could I beat the addiction? I noted the story of the temptation of Adam and Eve. The forbidden fruit was in the middle of the Garden of Eden—not in some obscure corner where they never saw it. It didn't seem to have any particular attraction to them until the serpent (I guess that was the devil) succeeded in getting them to focus their attention on the tree. Then it became something appealing and desirable (see Genesis 3:1–7). I reasoned that if they hadn't focused their attention on the forbidden fruit, they never would have eaten it. The first step, I concluded, was not to focus on the porn—either to look at it or try to avoid looking at it because either way I was thinking about porn.

Now trying to find application in the parable about the cleaned-out house, I remembered my mother's saying: "An idle mind is the devil's workshop!" I always thought that was just a way of keeping me busy, but now I realized that if I didn't take charge of what my mind was focusing on, the evil thoughts were more than ready to take center stage. So, I started lining up a bunch of things to think about when I wasn't forced to think about anything. I could sing a song in my mind, say a short prayer, recite some poetry, think about lines from a favorite movie, think of someone I could call and talk with or do some activity with, and so on. That really worked—for a while.

I fashioned in my mind the story of the shepherd boy David and the giant Goliath. Even though size-wise David was at a serious disadvantage—as I was with the monster pornography—he won the battle. I was confident I could do the same. I didn't anticipate that once I knocked my Goliath down, unlike David's Goliath, my Goliath would get up again and hit me hard. I suffered multiple relapses, although the time between episodes was getting longer and longer.

I just wanted to be free of the habit, but it seemed that I was too weak to knock out my Goliath once and for all. Then it dawned on me the Lord had said, "I will give you rest." Not that I could do it alone, but that with His help, I could gain the victory. I started—I would say "daily" but actually it was more minute by minute and then hour by hour—the habit of praying for divine assistance every time a thought to revert came to my mind. A quick prayer asking Jesus to help me out had a miraculous effect. Almost immediately I could sense an inner strength that I desperately needed to win the battle.

I did all the things everyone said to do—put my computer in a public place, block sites on my smart phone, avoid pornographic movies, and so on. Additionally, I took control of where I allowed my mind to focus. With the constant help of the Lord, I have been free for the past four years. Do I dare let down my guard? Not on your life. I know that Goliath can and will, at the first opportunity, resurrect and nail me as he had done so many times before.

What about the feelings of guilt I had suffered because I knew I was doing something that offended God? In time I realized that those nagging feelings were no longer gnawing at me. I no longer looked at women with that powerful lust I had formerly exhibited. Am I a saint? Hardly! But I don't have the same dread about meeting the Lord someday. I know that He helped me and continues to help me from falling back and allowing that darkness to extinguish the vision of what it feels like to walk in the Light.

Having taught college-age students for many years, I know that Ken's struggles are not unique. Both men and women continue to fall prey to the freedom-restricting chains of pornography. Rather than giving up in despair, as so many have, I believe that a loving, caring God is ready and willing to help anyone who asks for His help in overcoming this and any other undesirable habit or addiction. If we only look upwards and sensitively listen to His gentle invitation to "come unto me," I know He will respond.

POINTS TO PONDER

- Have you ever engaged in some innocent activity only later to discover that it has an addictive power you are struggling to master?
- Where have you found the most relief?
- Do you ever "relapse" after making some progress?
- How do you feel when you slip back again?
- Where do you look for permanent success?
- Have you included God in your quest to regain your freedom?
- Are you plagued with a sense of being controlled by some habit or substance?
- What are you willing to do to regain control?

3

MAKE THE BEST OF WHAT YOU HAVE

From Broken Body to Unbreakable Spirit

No legs, a riddled body, and a broken spirit. That is what Rick brought back from the Afghan war. Like so many other veterans, the impact the war left him with would follow throughout his life. Lying there alone in the army hospital bed looking down as his missing limbs, feeling an overwhelming darkness enveloping him, Rick had a decision to make. Were his injuries going to define who he was, or did he still have a future—even without legs?

The homecoming was emotional but also difficult. He hated being looked at as a cripple. His mind was still good, and he had full use of his upper body, including his arms. When people came to visit him and started showering him with sympathy, it made him mad rather than consoled him. He decided to use his physical condition as a tool rather than a crutch, an advantage rather than a handicap.

Using a scholarship the military makes available to veterans, and the money he received for his injuries, Rick enrolled in college. It wasn't easy at first. How was he to negotiate the steps to get to class? He said he had to swallow his pride, but when he asked, there was always one or two guys who would heist him up the stairs in his wheelchair. Most of his classrooms were wheelchair accessible. He had always prided himself in his upper body strength, so wheeling himself around campus wasn't a chore. Soon everyone seemed to recognize him and offered help when he needed it.

Contrary to what he had accepted as his likely lot in life, he found a girl who seemed to be able to look past his physical condition. They started dating, and just before he graduated with a social science degree, they were married. Now the challenge—how was he to support a wife? Was she going to be the breadwinner? His pride wouldn't even consider letting that happen. They both wanted to have a family, and she wanted to stay at home and guide the children through the difficulties of a deteriorating world.

Many nights were spent discussing their options. He could go into any number of trades since he was good with his hands. But he always had wanted to help people—that is why he had majored in social science. One day a former military buddy, now married and the principal of an elementary school, asked Rick to speak to his students about how to cope if your body isn't perfect. His friend had several handicapped students in his school, and he thought Rick could give them some hope for a normal future.

Rick prepared for the day, and when it came, it changed his life forever. As he sat in his wheelchair, the children sat on the floor gathered in a semicircle around him. He told them what happened when he stepped on a landmine. He had no trouble capturing their attention as he added the details of his injury, his hospital stay, and his looking down at where his legs used to be. He told of his decision not to allow his handicap to define or limit him. He told of his struggles to get an education, and date and marry his beautiful wife, who was standing behind him.

Then he opened it up for a question and answer period. He thought maybe one or two of the older children might ask a question. He was bombarded with dozens of questions. One little girl asked if he could still feel where his toes used to be. Everyone laughed when he said at times he did feel like his toes were still there. What was supposed to be a forty-five-minute presentation went for over two hours.

Rick knew where his future would take him. He said it was like God opened a door and showed him the endless vistas that awaited him if he was willing to take the risk and pay the price to go through the door.

Since that day some years ago, Rick and his wife have given hundreds of presentations to audiences from elementary schools, to college classes, to gatherings of veterans wounded in the war. Then came the day that they decided to start a foundation to help other wounded warriors. Because of Rick's willingness to be open and frank, his fame had spread. Donors came forth with contributions to his foundation. Before long there was more than sufficient funds to meet the demands of everyday living and provide some conveniences for Rick's growing family. He was able to quit his job and help others full-time.

If you were to ask him how he views his condition, he would tell you that he now looks at this injury as a blessing. He said if the bomb had not taken away his legs, he likely would have spent much more of his time in sports and fun, but non-essential, recreation. He also quickly adds that he and his wife and family enjoy many of the recreational activities that others do. He just does it from the confines of a wheelchair and without allowing recreation to control his life.

He said he tried prosthetic legs but, given the extent of his injuries, they hadn't worked for him. He tells of the time that he visited a wounded veteran in the hospital. The veteran was in a state of deep depression. He had the lower part of his right leg blown off and had resigned himself to a life of a cripple. When Rick wheeled himself into the room, with no legs, and talked with the wounded vet for an hour, he said the transformation was miraculous. Rick said he felt like God was directing him what to say. Thoughts he had never used before came to his mind. He said that many of the things he had planned to talk with the vet about didn't seem appropriate at the time.

Rick said that there were two miracles that day. One was the restored hope and optimism of the veteran, and the other was his recognition that God had a tailored message for each individual. Rick's former idea of "one size fits all" when counseling others was simply not true. He says that as he visits sick or wounded people now, he takes a few minutes and silently prays that he will be open to whatever inspired thoughts God wants the person to hear. He says he is beginning to feel more and more like a weak instrument in the hands of God in giving hope to the hopeless, help to those who need encouragement and guidance, and counsel to open up the windows of opportunity that God has for each of His spirit sons and daughters.

Rick is the first to admit that he isn't a perfect counselor. Sometimes the individual he is counseling isn't open to advice. He uses a trite cliché to express his frustration: "You can lead a horse to the water, but you can't make him drink!" That seems to be true with every problem that people face when others give heartfelt suggestions to help ease their burdens.

What does the future hold for Rick and his family? No one knows for sure, but Rick says he plans to continue "putting one foot in front of the other" (then he laughs), just trying to live one day at a time, taking full advantage of every opportunity to help and serve. He admits that some opportunities that require him to move outside his comfort zone are frightening. However, he is the first to tell you that with the help of God even the scariest things usually turn out better than expected.

Does he ever fail? He would say, "No, I just get another opportunity to try again and get it right." He claims that no setback needs to be permanent. With the help of God, all things are possible.

POINTS TO PONDER

- What if you, like Rick, were suddenly thrust into a physical condition that did not promise a complete recovery?
- Have you ever become angry at God, society, or others for your dilemma?
- How have you overcome that anger?
- Are you able to make the best of challenges life provides?
- What advice would you give a family member or friend who experiences such a challenge?

4

HOMELESSNESS—REALITY OR ILLUSION?

From Poverty to Peace

"Life on the streets isn't always a living hell—unless you consider where it ultimately ends," says Juan. There is no question that some people live on the streets and have no place for their permanent residence. However, virtually all of us are within one wildfire, one hurricane, one earthquake, one tsunami, or one tornado away from being homeless.

Juan shared his story about his discovery that homelessness for him was an illusion. It is true that Juan lived on the streets. Everything he owned was in a grocery cart. During the summers he slept in a park or on the sidewalk. In the colder months he sought refuge at a homeless shelter. He often ate the food that was discarded from restaurants. He seldom laundered his clothes and was quite content to live a life with little or no responsibility. After moving out of his parents' home, he had a job and an apartment. However, the pressure of meeting monthly rent and utility payments seemed like a dead-end road for him.

His friends, also homeless, reinforced each other. Each had a similar story, although the details varied. As long as he felt safe, Juan was content being homeless. Then came the day that he saw a family shopping for school clothes. The mother seemed very happy chasing after her two little children. The father was also attentive, laughing as the children played between stores. Suddenly a feeling of loneliness engulfed Juan. What was he missing in order to enjoy his carefree life?

He said he took stock of his situation that night and decided that the lifestyle he had chosen didn't have a very inviting ending. Some of his older companions had developed chronic diseases. As their health declined, there was no one to care for them or help meet their needs—only their homeless friends, many of whom were consumed with their own problems.

Juan had a living mother and father, a brother, and two sisters. He had turned his back on them when he decided to go homeless. He wondered if they would accept him if he chose to return. That thought haunted him for some time. Had they washed their hands of the son who had brought disgrace to the family? Juan started considering the impact his decision was having on his family.

During the years he had spent on the street, the only time God or Christ's name was mentioned was in a curse. Juan had been religiously inclined when he was growing up. What had happened? He realized that being a practicing Christian isn't a spectator sport. It requires a sustained effort and voluntarily taking on responsibility. Perhaps that is why he had run away from God.

Juan wondered to himself—he didn't dare openly discuss it with his homeless friends for fear of ridicule—if God would accept him if he straightened up his life. He had a lot to think about. Was he going to go cold turkey on the drugs, alcohol, and cigarettes? With no support group from his friends, would the challenge of cleaning up his life be too great? The darkness Juan felt in his mind and heart seemed to be escalating like an unchecked cancer. Something had to be done.

Finally, Juan decided to turn to God for help. That night, in the solitude of a dark alley, Juan knelt down and said the sincerest prayer he had ever offered. He recounts the feeling or impression that came to him. It was like a still small voice was saying, "Juan, you don't have a home on earth. That is of little matter. You will always have a home here with Me if you choose to respond to my invitation to come unto me!" Those words in his mind were so clear that he looked up to see if someone was there talking to him. It was still pitch dark around him, but he seemed to sense an inner light that confirmed that God really was aware of him and that He was willing to help him clean up his life. God was just waiting for Juan to look upward.

Juan didn't return to the company of his homeless buddies that night or ever again as a homeless man. He took the little he had and headed for home. It was, according to his story, a scary experience to approach his parents' home for the first time in several years. He wondered what his reception would be like. Several times he approached the door, but before knocking he retreated into the shadows of the foliage around the home. Finally, he mustered the courage to knock on the door. His father opened the door. At first he didn't recognize Juan. He was unshaven, dirty, and clothed in rags. However, as soon as his father recognized him, he immediately took him in his arms and wept on his shoulder. He called for his mother and siblings. They likewise embraced him and welcomed him home.

That night Juan slept in his old bed for the first time in years. A hot bath, a shave, and a change of clothing seemed to erase much of what had happened to him in the past years. That night before he drifted off to sleep, he thought about what had happened in the alley. Again, it was like a voice that said, "Juan, this is nothing to what it will be like when you return to My Home."

Juan's story doesn't end there. At first, he thought he would never return to his friends on the street. But he did return. Not to join them but to offer them the chance to change. Some of his friends, when they saw the change in Juan's appearance and the spirit he radiated, realized that they too could make the change. Some had no home to return to—that is, not here on earth. But as Juan told them of his alley experience and the recurrence of the experience the first night he was at his parents' home, that story seemed to resonate with some of his friends.

Others were not interested in changing. The ridicule he expected would happen did. He felt genuine sorrow for those who rejected his offer of help. Over the years Juan has continued to work with those who live on the streets.

I asked him about his opinion on whether homelessness was a reality or an illusion. He thought for a minute and said, "If you mean are there people who do not have a roof over their head or walls, windows, and doors to enclose them—yes. If you mean, are we ever truly homeless no matter of our earthly circumstances, I would answer no. We always will have an eternal home that we can strive to regain no matter what we have or do not have here on earth."

I have thought a lot about his answer. It is like being alone. We are never really alone. God is always there. We may not acknowledge Him or even believe in Him, but He never abandons us. Am I empathetic for those individuals who have chosen, either willingly or by force, to live on the streets? Absolutely. Do I wish I could provide housing for all of them? Of course. But my greater wish is that I could help develop faith and trust in the owner of our heavenly home and receive the immediate comfort that comes with that knowledge.

POINTS TO PONDER

- When you see people in undesirable conditions (like homelessness), do you tend to judge them without knowing the cause of their situation?
- How could you help someone who is in such a situation?
- Have you ever had to pull yourself out of an undesirable condition?
- What worked for you, and what didn't?
- Are you sensitively aware of how you feel when trying to decide which course to take?
- Can you discriminate between darkness and light when considering decisions you are forced to make?

5

THE GOD OF NATURE IS IN CONTROL

From Temptation to Trust

"Is Mother Nature trying to destroy me?" Probably, as in no other occupation is it more evident that man does not have complete control over his destiny than in occupations that depend on the God of nature. Having grown up in a farming community, although I am not a farmer, I was very aware that an early frost, lack of rain, a late freezing snowstorm, a hailstorm at the time of harvest, insufficient water to irrigate the crops, or any number of nature's unexpected and unwanted events could spell disaster for the farmer.

Ranchers weren't in any more secure a position. Lightning storms have sent flocks of sheep racing over a cliff to their deaths; cattle couldn't find sufficient feed to sustain themselves or their young; a flock of turkeys looked skyward during a heavy rainstorm and drowned (an event I actually witnessed). Ranchers too seemed helpless against the dirty tricks of Mother Nature.

When Mother Nature cooperated, farming and ranching provided a good income and the rewards of working with the land were soul-satisfying. But what about when things didn't go well? There are too many stories illustrating the point to focus on a single person's response. Let me summarize what I have observed and the lessons we can learn from them with two short vignettes.

One farmer in our community, Del, loudly proclaimed that he didn't believe in God and felt that it was strictly up to his genius if he prospered or not. He seemed to be one of the more prosperous farmers in the valley. One season things were looking very good for his acres of sugar beets. However, right at the time of harvest his son was killed when a tractor slipped out of gear and rolled over him. Del was devastated. He had relied heavily on his son. How could he possibly get the harvest done by himself?

He started the harvest, but it soon became evident that he wasn't going to get the crop harvested in time to make the company's deadline for receiving sugar beets. In desperation, and more to himself than to God, he cried heavenward for help. No voice, no vision, not anything came. That only seemed to confirm his belief that there was no God and he had to go it alone. All the other farmers were busy with their own harvest, so he didn't see how he could get the needed help in time.

Then, to his total amazement, half a dozen farmers showed up with their equipment. Each one said he had the strongest feeling that he should hurry and finish his harvest and go help Del. Each of the six said that their harvest had gone better and faster than ever before. So, without sacrificing their crops, they had come to rescue their neighbor. With the last load of sugar beets out of the ground and off to the factory, this case-hardened farmer sat on the top of a pile of sugar beet tops and wept.

He said he spent some hours thinking about what had happened. How could it be that such a coincident had occurred? None of the six rescuers had talked to the others before coming to help Del. They all came at about the same time (within an hour or two of each other). Their harvests had gone faster and better than ever before. As the sun went down, Del said he had the unmistakable impression that God had saved him, whereas at first he thought God didn't answer his prayer because nothing immediately happened. Now his thinking had changed. God didn't send angels to do his work for him. He just helped others put themselves in a position to help.

In years following this event, as he started looking for how God seems to answer farmers' prayers, this former atheist said, "I think God does hear us, knows our needs, but mostly answers our prayers through the actions of others."

I think Del's observation is correct. Sometimes the answers to prayers for help do not come. Such was the case with Harold, a sheepherder. The life of a sheepherder really doesn't lend itself to marriage and family life, so Harold was getting older but had never considered marriage.

According to his account, he had been running flocks of sheep on a certain range for some years. Although he always seemed to lose a few sheep to coyotes and wolves, generally he was able to keep his flocks safe and turn a profit at the end of the year.

This particular year, however, was different. It wasn't the predators that took its toll—it was disease. He did everything he knew how to do to stop the spread of the fatal disease, but to no avail. He said he prayed every night and morning and multiple times each day. Unfortunately, at the end of the year, very few sheep survived. He was ruined financially. He thought God had abandoned him. He had to move, and instead of being an owner he had to hire on as a sheepherder. That was a serious setback and a blow to his ego.

He moved to our valley for his new job. He was an excellent sheepherder and was soon recognized by the owner where he hired on as one with exceptional abilities. During the winter months, Harold had time on his hands and started attending the town dances and "shindigs," as they called them. There he met a woman who was single and had never married. Although she was attractive to him, she had passed what people normally call the marriageable age. Soon a romance blossomed, and before the next season when Harold would be gone to the range to herd sheep, they got married. Now instead of herding alone, Harold took his new bride with him. The small sheepherder's trailer would have seemed cramped to anyone else, but they were so much in love, according to their story, that the trailer seemed like a mansion.

During the summer, as they rode horses tending the sheep, they made plans on how to improve their lot. Donna, the new wife, had been frugal with her earnings even though she didn't have anything particular that she was saving for. They took Harold's earning for the year, combined it with Donna's savings and bought their own sheepherder's trailer and a small flock of sheep. Over time the flock multiplied, and soon they were further ahead than Harold had been before his devastating loss some years before.

If you talk with them, they will both say that if it hadn't been for Harold's setback in losing his flock of sheep, he never would have moved to our valley and would never have met Donna. Now he looks back and expresses thanks to a God who he claims orchestrated his failure in order to put him in a position to discover the love of his life. Was it just a coincidence? You would have a tough time convincing either Harold or Donna that it was a chance happening. Each would testify that God was in the details.

Sometimes, as with Harold and Donna, the results of the setbacks become readily identifiable. Other times, like with Del, it requires some serious analysis to see the hand of God in what has happened. Still other times it may not become apparent that God was there all the time and working behind the scenes to make life turn out for your best. Whatever the case may be, if you continue putting your trust in a real, personal, involved God, sooner or later you will see the benefit. Sometimes God deprives us of blessings only because He has greater blessings in store. Sometimes bad things (from our perspective) happen so that worse things that could happen are avoided. The key is to trust God and watch for the miracles.

POINTS TO PONDER

- Does blaming God ever bring a positive outcome?
- Are you prone to pass final judgment before playing out the situation and seeing what the end result is?
- Have you ever recognized God's answers to your prayers by the actions and interventions of others?
- Are there family or friends who could benefit from your example of courage and fortitude?
- Are there acquaintances who could use your help right now?

6

A VIOLATION OF A SACRED TRUST

From Abuse to Ambition

Janell is a beautiful eighteen-year-old. Her story elicits a range of emotions that are difficult to imagine. Her life started like all babies—loving parents, goofy but normal older brothers, a secure home, and little or nothing to worry about. However, her life took a drastic change. Here's her story:

At age eleven my life was turned upside down. I was just starting to show evidences of young womanhood. One night my father came into my bedroom and sat on the edge of the bed. He told me how beautiful I was and how quickly I was maturing into a young woman. I was a little taken aback because he had never talked to me like that before.

What he did next confused me and frightened me. He reached under my pajamas and rubbed my chest. I didn't know what to do. After all, he was my father. He had helped bathe me when I was very young, but nothing like this had ever happened before. He kissed me on the forehead and left. The next morning, I told my mother what had happened. She said not to worry about it. Likely it wouldn't happen again. But it did.

Almost nightly my father came into my bedroom after I was ready for bed. At first it was just lifting my pajama tops and exposing my breasts. Then he became progressively more intimate. All the time he was praising my beauty and telling me how irresistible I was. Then came the night that he pulled my pajama bottoms down, exposing my genitals. I was horrified. Again, I told my mother what was happening and she just blew it off. She did nothing to stop it.

You can probably guess the rest of the story from here. The first time he raped me was something that caused nightmares for years. I hadn't yet turned twelve. I felt dirty. I felt violated. I felt betrayed. Here was a man who was duty-bound to protect me, and he was using me like a common woman of the streets. I cried myself to sleep so many nights I can't begin to number them. Three, maybe four, times a week the ritual was reenacted. There was no use resisting or he would get angry and hit me. I thought my world had come to an end. However, that was just the beginning.

On one of the nights my father didn't come to my bedroom, my oldest brother came in. He said he knew what was going on between me and Dad and wanted the same treatment. I told him "no" as emphatically as I could. He wasted no time tearing off my clothes and raping me. Again, I told my mother but received the same "couldn't-care-less" response. I was trapped and had no way out.

Over the next three years, until I was fourteen, my father and my three brothers used me whenever they wanted to. I had numbed myself because the pain of thinking about what was happening to me was too great to bear. I knew I had to get out of there. I knew there had to be justice somewhere. But where?

My family had once been church-goers. I remember when I was six or seven years old singing songs in Sunday School about how God loves little children. I decided if I couldn't get any relief and help from the people around me, I would try getting God to help me. That night, after what seemed like the nightly abuse, I got down on my knees and pleaded with God to help me. I wish I could say that an angel came down with a big sword and exacted justice on my father and brothers, but it didn't happen that way.

About a week later, a woman came to my school to talk to my class about sexual abuse. She said there were places girls and women could go to escape the abusers. After the talk, I followed her to the foyer and asked if she could tell me of a place I could go. She immediately took my hand, led me to her car, and drove me to a shelter. The counselor at the shelter talked with me for a long time, getting as many details as I was willing to give.

With the help of the administrators at the shelter, I was taken to a location far from my home. They said they would alert my family that I had left and if they tried to find me, they would make sure the police were informed what they had been doing. They said they would assure them that a very long prison life lay ahead of all of them if they wanted to pursue the matter.

Somehow, I thought God would just step in and straighten them around so we could have a normal family. As I look back, now four years later, I can see that God was helping me all the way along. First, He numbed me so I could live with what was happening. Then He put me in a class where sexual abuse was talked about in an informing but non-threatening way. Then He helped me find the shelter where I could get away from the hell I had lived in for the past four years.

I guess my story could end with getting away and living in a safe haven. However, I don't know exactly how it happened—probably the administrators at the shelter set up the meeting—but a very wealthy man heard of my situation. He arranged a meeting between me, the counselor at the shelter, and him. He asked what I wanted to do with my life. I told him I wanted to become an attorney so I could prosecute my family for what they had done to me. It blew me away when he said he wanted to finance my entire education all the way through law school. Next year, I will start my undergraduate work. With his help, I will make good my desire to get a law degree.

However, yet another change is taking place that is totally unexpected. I can only attribute it to God working behind the scenes. Each day as I dream about college, it seems that my goal for getting a law degree is becoming less pressing for the purpose of getting even with my family. Perhaps God is saying, "Let me take care of your family in My own way. Eventually the scales of justice will be leveled—to your complete satisfaction. But if you let the spirit of revenge you now have keep gnawing away at you, you are giving your family power to stop your progress. Too much of your time and mental energy is being eaten up in trying to be their judge. I will be the Judge."

Of course, God is right—He is always right. Now the decision to put the past behind me and move ahead is taking center stage of my mind. My focus is still on getting a law degree but with an emphasis on being an advocate and protecting women's rights. Talking with other women and girls at the center, I realize that recovering and moving on is an individual matter. Some who are abused may take a lifetime to fully recover; others move on rather quickly. Recovering is not only an individual matter but a very complex process. My suggestion is to get help as quickly as possible and start the healing process.

What about marriage in the future? I believe I will marry when the right guy comes along. I will not allow the abuse to rob me of my dreams of being a wife and a mother. They may have robbed me of my innocence, but since I was an unwilling participant in the abuse, I feel I still have my virtue intact. I can't begin to express how light and happy I feel. If everyone could feel what I am feeling now, the whole world would be heaven on earth. I thank God multiple times every day for being patient with my feelings for revenge and patiently turning me toward the Light—Jesus Christ.

What can I add to Janell's story? From the depths of hell she caught a glimpse of celestial Light. Each of us, no matter what our earthly hell is like, can know that the same God who lifted Janell is there for you and me as well.

POINTS TO PONDER

- Does it seem that there is no justice between the bookends of birth and death?
- Have you considered that the scales of justice might not be perfectly balanced in this life?
- How have you coped when things are not fair?
- Have you ever considered helping others who have been violated or wronged?
- How would you counsel someone like Janell?

7

HAPPILY EVER AFTER? DELUSION OR POSSIBILITY?

From Contention to Connection

So help me God! That sounded like such a strange way to end a wedding ceremony. However, like any number of couples, Mel and Sofi started their marriage with all the optimism, dreams, and hopes for a perfect marriage. According to Sofi's account, with frequent interruptions and injections by Mel, this is how it unfolded.

We met at a church barbecue. It was like love at first sight. We had a whirlwind courtship, and the minister gladly performed the wedding ceremony. It seemed a little strange to both of us that he put so much emphasis on the words "so help me God!" That wouldn't become relevant until some years had passed.

The early years of our marriage mirrored what we had heard of other couples—fun, excitement, enjoying each other physically, socially, and spiritually. We were regular church attenders before marriage and continued after. Our minister was funny, motivational, and had some good practical advice. He and his wife were what we wanted to become.

Before long we started our family. Introducing a baby into our relationship changed things. I spent a lot of nights walking the floor with a colicky baby. I knew Mel needed the sleep because of his demanding job. In retrospect we both agree Mel should have been more sensitive to my needs. The 24/7 demands of the baby were taking their toll. I was a bit short tempered, didn't keep myself dolled up like I always had, and I was too tired and not motivated so I let the house fall into disarray. I started to resent Mel. He was leaving everything up to me as though I were a domestic servant.

I tried to mention my plight to Mel, but it seemed that every time I made a suggestion, he took offense and would fire back at me with one of my apparent flaws. Instead of working together to solve the problem, I started to go silent, avoiding the increasingly frequent fights and escalating attacks on each other. Of course, none of this happened overnight. Gradually we became two people living under the same roof but sharing few common interests other than our increasing family. Even our intimate times were less frequent and not enjoyable. Mel admitted that he made a stupid mistake—adding to all the others we were making. With the decreased satisfaction of sex in our marriage, he turned to the internet for some "pseudo-thrills." He didn't do it frequently, but it certainly didn't help the situation. I felt betrayed and useless.

If it hadn't been for the children, we would have divorced and looked for greener pastures elsewhere. But we knew that joint custody would have devastated the kids, and neither of us wanted to miss out on their growing up. Unfortunately, without us realizing it, our bickering and fighting was beginning to be mirrored by our children. Their fights were small and sometimes humorous at first. But as time when on, they sounded as ugly and sarcastic as we did when we argued. It was pretty obvious to both of us that life couldn't go on like this.

As I mentioned, we were attending church services regularly. We were "there" but "not there." We listened to the sermons—many of which had a lot of good advice and some good humor—but we never discussed if we should try what we had heard. There was a darkness that had entered our marriage that neither of us had experienced before. Whenever I would suggest we make some changes, Mel's stupid pride (what he called it!) wouldn't allow him to humble himself, admit I was right, and take steps to fix the situation.

One particular Sunday the clouds foreshadowing the approaching storm were so dark we had to use the headlights on our way to church. It was like the darkness surrounding us mirrored the penetrating darkness within us. We drove in silence to church.

What happened next changed the course of our entire lives. The bombshell came that Sunday when we arrived at church and a new minister was there. He explained that our old minister and friend had divorced his wife and moved to a different town. We were blown away! How could this man of God, this sterling example of everything we wanted to become, who had given so many wonderful sermons on how to be happy in marriage, possibly do this? We left church that day devastated. If our minister couldn't make a go of marriage, how could we?

On the way home, I had the strongest impression. I remembered the minister's emphasis at our wedding ceremony: "So help me God!" It was like a bolt of lightning. That was our problem. We had heard all the sermons and the scriptures telling us, "Be ye therefore perfect even as your Father in Heaven is perfect" (Matthew 5:48) and the frequent invitation of the Lord: "Come follow me." But we hadn't done that! We hadn't asked God to help us! One of the last sermons the minister gave was entitled "God Is Love" (1 John 4:16). It didn't take a PhD in theology to realize that if either or both of us did something that caused God to withdraw from our marriage, then love would diminish.

For the first time in years, we had a heart-to-heart talk. We put our foolish pride aside and did something we should have been doing for years—we actually talked with God. We had "said our prayers," but I'm afraid my prayers hadn't gone beyond the ceiling. This time we really prayed. It wasn't like we heard a voice or saw an angel. It was more like our minds were opened up and we received a flood of impressions of things we needed to fix if our marriage was to last and our family was to stay together.

We had fallen into the habit of looking for the flaws we thought we saw in each other. As one would criticize, the other would retaliate with increasing bitter accusations. One of the first impressions we got was that we needed to go back to a practice we had when we first got married—look for the positive and compliment each other. Another impression was that we needed to serve each other, do the kind things for each other we used to do, and be more interested in meeting our spouse's needs rather than selfishly wanting all of our needs met. We remembered the Lord's teaching about the mote we thought we saw in the other's eyes and how He counseled us to remove the beam from our own eyes first.

This commitment to change started in a nanosecond, but we messed up a lot and had to start all over again. But each time we fell, we didn't seem to fall as far, so we could start from a higher position. As we focused on eliminating those habits we had fallen into and replacing them with practices we wanted in our marriage and family, we noted an increase in love for each other. It was like when we invited God into our marriage, He brought love with Him. We were almost like newlyweds again.

Church became a new experience for us. Rather than just listening to the words of the sermons, we started taking notes on how we could apply the principles in our lives. It was like someone turned on the light and we could see issues and problems more clearly. That brought church to a new level for us. We also noted that the more we used the things we were learning in our marriage, the more we started looking at others in a more positive light. We stopped criticizing the faults we thought we saw in others and started complimenting their good points. It was almost like a miracle. People really warmed up to us. We started making really good friends with people at church and in the neighborhood.

Were we perfect? No, we messed up a lot. Some people thought we had an ulterior motive. We really tried to be sincere. Even our children noticed the difference. They still had their little fights, but not the ugly, intense battles they had engaged in before. What did we learn? We learned that God really is Love and where God's Spirit is, love is there. When we do or say things that offend God, love diminishes. That seems to be the key to how we know we are doing okay. If God's Spirit is with us, we're okay. If it isn't, we are not okay. No use kidding ourselves. We are the losers if His Spirit departs.

As I write this vignette, I can see that I have made many of the same mistakes. Now it is time to practice what I preach—walk the walk rather than just talk the talk. It is never too late to recapture those intense feelings of love you had when you decided to marry. It just requires the swallowing of some pride, admitting you've got some improving to do, and—most important—inviting God (Love) into your marriage. As the three of you work on your relationship, you will discover a depth to your marriage you didn't even know was possible.

POINTS TO PONDER

- Have you experienced a decrease in love in your marriage and family with the passage of time?
- What can you do to recapture that love and optimism you had when you were first married?
- Have you considered having a regular "reality check" in marriage to identify and eliminate divisive habits?
- Have you tried talking to other couples who seem to be living "happily ever after"? What are their suggestions?
- Have you tried praying together as a couple and asking for divine help?
- Have you tried looking for the positive in each other while working to overcome the irritations?

8

POLITICIAN-AWAKENING FROM A DEEP SLEEP

From Insecurity to Integrity

"Politicians are not perfect people!" That statement started an interesting conversation I had with a man who formerly served in the House of Representatives in Washington DC. An abridgement of his story follows:

I was determined to go to Washington and make a difference. The campaigning was difficult, but the vision of the changes I could effect drove me on. In a bitterly conducted campaign where more lies were told about me than I imagined possible, I finally succeeded and won the election.

At first, I was overwhelmed with the halls of Congress. There were places I had only heard about or seen on television. The first few months were eye-opening experiences. I witnessed firsthand how the system worked or, more accurately, didn't work. I saw good men and women really trying to make a difference. Others seemed to have lost their direction and were more interested in getting noticed on national media and using their office for personal gain.

Halfway through my first term I realized that more and more often I was taking sides on issues not based on what my constituents wanted but what I personally wanted. I found that I was being courted by lobbyists on every issue that came before the House. The pressure was unreal. Some of the lobbyists suggested that they could make it "worth my while" if I voted in a certain way. I had heard of corruption among the congressmen, but now I was seeing it firsthand. Not all of the elected officials accepted bribes or perks, but many did.

I noticed that some lawmakers didn't even read the laws they were voting on. "Pass it and we'll find out what it says later" was more than a humorous slogan. Other lawmakers legislated for their own districts with no concern on the impact on the rest of the country. Often, they would tie their bills to larger, more popular bills. When the popular ones passed, their selfish laws were passed also.

Another disappointing practice I observed was the number of congressmen who didn't show up to vote on important bills. Even if they showed up to vote, often they had not taken the time or expended the energy to really understand the bills. It was difficult to see how many lawmakers were on personal vacations when important votes were scheduled.

Probably the most distressing was the partisan politics that was divisive. Bills that would benefit the entire nation were either voted down or not brought to a vote because of the unwillingness of one party to cooperate with the other party. Even issues that had been strongly supported but a few years back were voted against when brought to the floor when the opposing party was in power.

The longer I served, the more difficult it became to resist the pressure. I had developed close friends in the Congress, so when they implored me to vote one way or the other, even if I didn't agree with the bill, I felt obligated to align with them. I knew in some future bill I would want them to support me. That isn't all bad unless you are voting on a bill that you have strong feelings is not in the best interest of the people of the country.

As to my resolve to clean up the corruption in Washington—well, that soon became a dream that I knew I couldn't accomplish. I saw one legislator get "some dirt" on another lawmaker and then literally blackmail him into voting on a certain proposed bill. I never tried to tally up the honest lawmakers from those who were there for their own good. I think the answer would have been very disappointing.

One night I was lying awake thinking about an important bill that was to be brought to the floor the next day. It was one of those bills where every vote counts and was destined to be decided by one or two votes. Everyone knew that my vote would likely be the one that determined whether it passed or failed. I knew there were loopholes in the bill that could be exploited by corrupt politicians at some future date. My gut told me to vote against it, but I knew the ridicule I would take from my colleagues and from the national press. The pressure was unbearable.

I must have dozed off and fallen into a fitful sleep. I tossed and turned as the dreams or nightmares bombarded me one after the other. Then a dream came that was so real I couldn't tell whether I was asleep or awake. In this dream I was standing in a large hall like the one the House of Representatives meets in. But instead of my fellow legislators in the seats, the Lord was in the chairman's seat. The other seats were filled with angels in glistening white robes. All of them were staring intently at me.

The Lord reviewed the proposal I was to vote on. The implications were laid out in perfect clarity. The devastating abuse of the loopholes was made known. I noted that I was sweating profusely, knowing that mine was the deciding vote. There was dead silence as I tried to explain the pressure I was feeling, the ridicule I would receive if I voted against the bill, the negative press who would devour me like a piece of raw meat, and on and on. But each time I made an excuse to bolster my decision to vote for the bill, the very sound of my explanation sounded so lame and unimportant.

The dream closed without my making known my decision. The next day, with all eyes focused on me, I cast my vote against the bill. The oppositions' voices were as loud and condescending as I had expected. The national press was as vicious as I had known they would be. But I had a strange calm inside me. I knew I had made the right decision.

I opted not to run for re-election. I still am very interested in politics and want to make a difference. But I have decided to work from the outside rather than as an elected official. And, just as a point of interest, history has proven that I was right in voting against that bill. Further debate, as the opposition tried to overturn the vote, proved to be very insightful. Many of the factors influencing me to vote against the bill seemed to convince other lawmakers of the inadvisability of the bill.

As I have pondered the ramifications of his explanation, I have wondered if our great lawmakers have failed to consider what God has revealed as they deliberate the mountain of bills they are considering. It seems the further we stray from what God has revealed in making and enforcing laws, the worse the conditions are for us as a nation. A final thought: The scriptures say that everyone will be judged according to the deeds done in the flesh (see Revelation 20:12–14). I wonder if our great lawmakers are aware that the day will come when they will be asked to account for the laws they passed and the influence wielded while serving as representatives of the people. If they realized that, would they be more careful how they used their influence?

POINTS TO PONDER

- Have you thought about how broad your influence might be?
- Have you ever observed others who used their positions of power to build themselves but not to benefit those they represent?
- How can you avoid making the same mistake?
- Is it okay to use your position of power to influence others?
- Are there times when you should go against the voice of the majority?
- What criteria can you use to determine when your insight trumps the voice of the people?

9

FINDING GOD FOR THE FIRST TIME

From Foreign to Familiar

My wife and I recently had the opportunity of spending some time in Australia. What a wonderful country and a delightful people. We were there over the Christmas holiday. Australia is not noted for being a religious country, but they are definitely gracious people. It is also a country of diverse cultural backgrounds.

Many of the people we met, especially the Asians, spoke little or no English. Observing their devotion to family and their traditions caused me to wonder if America, in trying to be so progressive, is losing a valuable part of our heritage.

I wish I could let the participant in this activity explain what happened it in his own words, but he spoke no English and I speak no Chinese. This is what I observed.

One of the local churches put on a Christmas display starting with a large, back-lit mural of the Savior. The Nativity scene was portrayed with life-sized camels and wise men, the visit of the Angel Gabriel, the birth of the Christ Child, and the manger scene. An adjacent room had several paintings by a variety of artists depicting different events in Christ's life. Those sponsoring the display said that more than ten thousand people come to view the display each year. Many of the visitors were Chinese people who lived nearby but knew nothing of God, Jesus, or Christianity in general.

Each night a bilingual guide was there to explain in their language what each display represented. I was there one evening when a Chinese family came to view the display. The guide explained that Jesus is our loving Brother who lived a perfect life and then laid down His life for us so we could be resurrected after we die. He also explained that Jesus' Father was God, a personal Being who loves us and wants us to return to live with Him forever.

The reaction of the man, particularly, but the whole family together was like someone had turned on a light in the darkened room where they had been living their whole lives. I assume it is Chinese tradition for the husband to take the lead in discussions. The father began asking questions as quickly as the guide could answer them. The family had never heard such a story and wanted to know more. They were like sponges soaking up everything that was said.

Several times the father asked if the guide would repeat the part about God being a personal, loving God. The family wanted to know if they could go into the chapel on the property and see God. They wanted to know what resurrection meant. They seemed really interested in the idea that their ancestors who had passed away were alive in a spirit world and would someday meet them again. They wanted to know if there were any books or materials that would explain further what they were hearing for the very first time.

Rather than rush through the display as I normally would have because I know the story well, I decided to hang around in the background and follow the family through the various exhibits. It was heartening to see them point at different items in the displays, like the camels and the Angel Gabriel, and chatter in Chinese, demonstrating their excitement and interest. While most visitors completed the tour in about fifteen to twenty minutes, this family was there for well over an hour. I only wish I could have understood their language and tried to help answer their questions.

As my wife and I returned to our hotel, I thought how different the Chinese family's reaction was from so many others who had heard all the stories about God and Christ but showed little or no interest in learning more. I thought of the billions of people living in countries where Christianity, if present at all, has only a minuscule presence.

I lay awake that night pondering the question: "What difference would it make to me if any and all ideas of God and Christ were withdrawn from my life?" As I did a summary of my life, I could see that virtually every part of my life was influenced by my belief in a Supreme Being. The way I acted toward my wife and family and others was molded by my belief that Christ had revealed the keys to happy living. I could hardly begin to comprehend what my life would be like without a belief in God and Christ.

After determining that my life would only be a shell of what it is now without God and Christ being involved in it, I wondered about my many friends who have chosen to distance themselves from God. Did they sense the same emptiness I envisioned would exist in my life? What did they see without God and Christ that was so appealing that they could turn their backs on what they formerly believed? Were they settling for fleeting thrills of worldly pleasures without considering the impact of living without God eternally?

I thought of the children of those who have turned away from God. What was the likelihood that their parents would teach them about God and Christ? Would the parental influence make atheists or at least agnostics of the next generation? What impact would that have on the laws that our children passed? Would their lack of moral absolutes allow social practices to become socially acceptable when they were formerly forbidden by divine command but accepted as normal because of their upbringing?

Then a startling thought entered my mind: "I am living to witness the very destruction of society that I envisioned would happen if people abandoned their faith in God and Christ." Rather than accept that God created mankind, male and female, after His own image, modern man has determined that anyone can choose whether they want to be male or female. We seem to be living in a world Isaiah saw thousands of years ago when he said modern man would "turn everything upside down" (Isaiah 29:15–16). He further cautioned: "Woe unto them that call evil good, and good evil; that put darkness for light, and light for darkness; that put bitter for sweet, and sweet for bitter!" (Isaiah 5:20).

I wondered if the turmoil, anger, and violence we are watching escalate at an alarming rate is directly tied to our progressive abandonment of God-revealed principles. It may be in the coming years that those billions who have not been introduced to God, Christ, and Their gospel will be the ones who step forth and save mankind from the suicidal course we seem to be taking.

When I think of the enthusiasm and interest the Chinese family exuded, I wonder if we could regain that same enthusiasm we once had for God, if we would recover our belief in God and Christ and begin to align our lives with Their revealed plan for our happiness. If we continue to pick up the stick of carnal gratification, we can hardly expect that lasting happiness and peace will be on the other end of the stick. The abandonment of moral principles has never brought lasting happiness, and it never will.

POINTS TO PONDER

- Do you use yourself as the standard to judge other people?
- Is it all right to share your beliefs without being pushy or overbearing?
- How can you allow people to differ from you without becoming argumentative?
- Do you have beliefs or values you feel worthy of sharing?
- How can you talk about your beliefs without coming across as fanatical?

10

THE WORST MISTAKE OF MY LIFE

From Deceit to Dedication

Unfortunately, this scenario is replayed daily in everyday life. I have taken this example from my personal experience with two families I know and love. I'll let George tell the story in his own words:

I was living the ideal life—beautiful wife, smart kids, a good job, lots of friends, good health, and anything else you want to include in that heaven-like relationship. My wife and I had been married for thirteen years and were still very much in love. I had worked my way up in my company to a managerial position. One of our long-serving secretaries retired, and a younger woman was hired to replace her. She was attractive, personable, intelligent, professional, and a good worker. We developed a friendly professional relationship.

Then things began to change. It started so innocently. We went to lunch together—just the two of us. We talked business and made some serious progress on a project I was in charge of that had stalled. We concluded that working closely together in a more relaxed environment helped move my projects along.

Little did either of us realize that the professional relationship we enjoyed was slowly turning into a romantic relationship. After several months, with both of us having been in denial, we admitted that we had feelings for each other. We discussed what to do about it but didn't come to a firm conclusion. As the lunch dates continued, the physical attraction continued to escalate. One day we were alone in the elevator from the cafeteria to our office on the ninth floor, and we exchanged an affectionate kiss.

That was the beginning of what quickly escalated into episodes of increased intimacy. Kissing and cuddling soon gave way to caressing and fondling. We both knew it was wrong, but it was so satisfying that neither of us wanted to quit. Then came the final blow. We were assigned to take a three-day business trip to a distant city to close a lucrative business deal. We had different hotel rooms that were adjacent to each other. Everything was all right the first night, but on the second and third nights we stayed in the same room, shared the same bed, and committed the act intended only for husbands and wives.

We were ashamed and heartbroken. We decided not to tell our spouses about what had happened and vowed not to repeat the mistake. So much for the resolve. Over the next number of months, we secretly met for sex on multiple occasions. Finally, the guilt we both were experiencing was too great to bear. We each told our spouses and filed for divorces so we could marry.

I can't describe the pain I caused my wife and children. It seemed so right at the time. But after the divorce and marriage, things went downhill. My children wanted nothing to do with me. The love we had shared for a lifetime rapidly turned into loathing toward me. Even though I was granted visitation rights, the few times they did happen were cold and hurried. The kids couldn't get away from me fast enough. My new wife was suffering through a similar experience.

I can't tell you how many times we discussed whether we had made a terrible mistake. But the deed was done and we were living with the consequences. So guilty did we feel that we opted not to include prayer, scripture reading, and church attendance in our new life. In retrospect, that really accelerated the decline of spirituality and peace we had both enjoyed with our former spouses and family.

It didn't take long to realize that the love we thought we had was diminishing, and eventually feelings of affection for one another died. Not finding the happiness we thought we would have, we fell into the same ugly pattern that had resulted in our first divorce. I found another married woman who was in a troubled marriage. My wife, still a very attractive woman, had no trouble becoming intimate with a married man. Three divorces resulted.

My third marriage didn't last long. Soon I was divorced again and determined to remain single. As I sat alone in a dingy, rented apartment, I wondered if I had a soul that could be redeemed. It seemed every relationship I touched became like rotten fruit. In desperation, I got on my knees and for the first time in years pleaded with the Lord for some help to get my life back on track. I felt like a total hypocrite talking with God since I had broken His commandments and turned my back on the truths that I knew by personal experience had brought me such joy and happiness.

I didn't experience an immediate sense of relief, but I was determined not to give up. I did feel a spark like a match that starts a fire. I returned to the activities that had brought such peace and joy before I had strayed. I started praying multiple times every day, and I read the Bible daily. I even started attending church meetings again, but I have to admit I was very uncomfortable at first. I mistakenly thought everyone knew everything I had done and was silently condemning me.

I was single for well over a year before I regained some confidence in my ability to live a good Christian life. Over time I felt the light come back into my life. The darkness that had clouded my vision began to dissipate. I can't remember the exact day or time when I felt like I regained a sure knowledge that God was there for me. He knew me by name, had forgiven me of my sins, and was willing to tutor me back onto the straight and narrow path.

I'm still hesitant to enter into another marriage. Perhaps in time that will come. I haven't tried to keep up with the other wives other than noting that their experience paralleled my own. I wondered how the Lord would compensate for the trail of misery and heartache I had made.

I discovered that my first wife had married a man who treated her with the respect she deserved. I couldn't believe how my children had matured. Unfortunately, I have no relationship with them. Why did I do what I did? Where did I make my first mistake? I have asked myself those questions and a boat load of others many times over the years. How different my life would have been if I had honored my marital vows and been wise enough to take steps to avoid the romantic feelings when they first became apparent. However, that door was closed. But contrary to what I thought, the Lord has allowed me to pick myself up again (with His help), and try again to find happiness and success in this life.

My advice to all those who think that extra-marital affairs are okay, is DON'T DO IT! It may be thrilling and exciting at first, but the inescapable results of going down that path are not pleasant or desirable. For me and for many others I know about, that detour is short-lived and ends in a soul-destroying cliff at the end.

The message of hope is that there is a way back. It isn't easy and is one to be avoided at all costs. But I have come to know firsthand that there is a God in heaven who knows me and is willing to help me achieve all He has in store for me if I am willing to humble myself and play by His rules.

POINTS TO PONDER

- Have you experienced such a scenario?
- What did you do to prevent the devastation George experienced?
- What would you do if you saw a friend or co-worker engaging in that kind of life-destroying activities?
- Do you sense any obligation to help others avoid the trap?
- What lessons have you learned from the experience of others?

11

LESSONS LEARNED ABOUT BUSINESS BY WATCHING GOD

From Profit to Purpose

Warren is a successful businessman by all standards. He has a robust company employing many workers. He has carved out a significant niche in his market and is in the process of diversifying. However, during our conversation attempting to identify the elements contributing to his success, he made some insightful observations:

For the first few years in business, I was working what seemed like 24/7. The measure of our success depended solely upon the bottom line—how much profit we made. All of our attention was directed toward streamlining production, cutting the costs of materials we were using, and making sure our method of distribution was fine tuned.

Personally, I began to feel trapped in the business. I wasn't enjoying life, no matter how much profit we turned. I found myself having to force myself to go to work. It felt like a depressive cloud was hanging over my head. In the midst of all this I noted that the turnover in our employees continued to escalate. What was wrong? We were paying good wages, had good benefits, good paid vacation, and other perks that we thought would be appealing to our workers. Yet they were leaving at the very time they got to the point of being valuable to the company.

After a lot of soul-searching, I did what I have done over my lifetime—I turned to God. I spent many hours in silent meditation mentally dissecting every aspect of my business, looking for weaknesses that I could fix or anything I had overlooked. Almost like a thought from outer space, the question came: What does God do strictly for Himself? I had never considered that. Upon closer investigation I concluded that virtually everything God did was for the benefit and progress of His spirit children—mankind. His satisfaction and joy must be tied to His efforts to make available opportunities for mankind to progress and grow.

That was one glaring deficiency in the policies of my company. Everything was for the benefit of the company. The financial and other perks we were providing for our employees did not automatically translate to their personal growth and the achievement of their life goals. To say that presenting this idea to our senior management team was a shock would be an understatement. Their exchanged glances and quizzical looks communicated their confusion and possibly suggested their questioning my mental stability.

It took some time to flesh out what we needed to do. The head of each of our divisions was given the assignment to find out what every one of their employees wanted to achieve in their lifetime. If they saw their position in my company as a mere temporary position until they could find something better and more fulfilling, we had to know that. We wanted them to view their position in our company as the beginning of a lifelong commitment as we tried to help them achieve their goals.

Almost immediately as we implemented the new philosophy, employee turnover began to decrease. Instead of our employees seeing employment as a job, they began to expand their vision and see that any efforts to build the company was a means for furthering their progress toward their goals. Did we still have employee turnover? Yes, but when they left it was because they had arrived at a point where they felt they could take the next step in achieving their goal. None of the employees departed with a negative attitude. Rather, they left expressing their appreciation in helping them see their potential and how to achieve it.

When the emphasis changed from measuring success depending on the bottom line to the personal growth of our employees, we noted that the bottom line also improved. There was more of a family feeling among the employees. When an employee was struggling either with his assigned task or even with personal or family problems, other employees seemed willing to jump in and help him succeed.

It would be incorrect to suggest that everything changed immediately and now our company was running perfectly. We still have our challenges, our employee discontent, and our interpersonal problems, but our approach to coping with the problems has changed. Additionally, my enthusiasm for work returned and the depressive cloud dissipated. Instead of viewing all of our challenges as bad, we started looking at them as necessary areas to focus on in order to solve the problem and turn the negative into a positive.

Where we used to celebrate the profit for the month, now we celebrated the employee of the month. And rather than limiting the award to a single employee, we chose to honor all those who excelled in their position. Sometimes we would have a dozen employees receiving the monthly award—and that came with financial and other perks.

As I continued to analyze how God interfaced with mankind, I realized that one person's success did not limit others from succeeding. There was more room at the top than a single spot for a superstar. I also concluded that one failure or mistake by a person did not result in God's firing him. God seemed more than willing to help the struggling person get back on his feet and try again. More often than not, according to my own experience when I had stumbled either in business or in my family relationship, I was not only able to repent but also was given additional insights to help me avoid making the same mistake in the future.

Again, based on my own experience, I noted that God didn't jump in and fix my problems but was willing to inspire me to know how to solve the problem. Rather than complaining about how difficult the problems were, I began to see them as greater opportunities to learn God-like principles. I can't count the number of mistakes I made along the way, but none of them were fruitless when I used them to learn how to do it better.

I noted that the unity among members of my executive team seemed to translate into more contentment and greater enjoyment among the employees under them. It was not a pleasant experience when, after multiple attempts to correct the problem, I had to let one of my vice presidents go. He just couldn't or wouldn't accept the directions we were trying to go. Not without precedence, I noted how some of the Lord's disciples turned away from Him when He introduced some difficult doctrine that they wouldn't accept (see John 6:66–67).

One thing I also noted in my attempts to learn from God's example is that His success is not inextricably tied to the success or failure of His children. His happiness and success seem to be knowing that He has given His children every opportunity and every resource necessary for their success based on each individual's capacity. Not all of mankind have equal abilities. In giving talents to His servants, the Lord gave one ten talents, another five talents, and another one talent. Then at the time of accounting, he rewarded those who used their talents to increase and improve. Each was given like commendation while the servant who squandered his talent was stripped of his talent and cast out. Read the account in Matthew 25:14–30.

I could go on and on in my analysis, but what I have said will probably give you enough meat to chew on as you analyze what we can learn from God about being successful in a business or in our lives or with our families.

I heartily endorse what Warren has suggested and hope you will continue comparing your methods of doing business with how God administers His world and try to mimic His principles.

POINTS TO PONDER

- Have you considered looking at God as the Master Employer?
- Can you use some of the things the Lord demonstrated in how He handled different kinds of situations with a variety of people?
- Are some principles of working with people the same no matter when in earth's history they happen?
- Could you improve your work, marriage, or family by searching out those never-changing principles?
- Has your marriage, career, work, or profession become a drudgery rather than interesting and challenging?
- Have you pondered how you might reverse the trend and recapture the excitement you once enjoyed?

12

POINT OF NO RETURN

From Indulgence to Investment

Joe is a unique character. He grew up a devote Christian, joined the Army, and followed the course that many service people do in abandoning all sense of morality. He was discharged, got a job, got married, and then allowed his life to spiral out of control with drugs, alcohol, pornography, sex, virtually anything he wanted to do. According to his account he was searching for happiness in all the wrong places. His portrayal of what happened is best described using his own words:

After the military and marriage, I felt I had discovered what was making me unhappy. It was all of the rules and restrictions that are expected if a person wants to be a practicing Christian. I decided to make my own pathway to happiness. I turned my back on God. Anything He said to do, I chose to do the opposite.

At first every new activity was thrilling. In retrospect I think it was in doing of something I knew to be wrong that the real thrill or rush came. However, in time I realized that I had to go further and further into the darkness to get the same sense of excitement. It never crossed my mind that my denying there was a God and that there would someday come a day of judgment did nothing to erase the fact that God exists and that someday every person on earth would stand before Him to be judged of the things they did on earth.

I can't remember exactly when or how it happened that I found myself staring into the black hole of hopelessness and fearing that I had crossed the point of no return. It seemed like in a nanosecond all the thrills and excitement that I had experienced as I plunged downward disappeared. There was nowhere else to go, nothing else I could do to get what I now realized was a false promise by a very evil devil. I could almost hear the devil laughing at my stupidity and loudly proclaiming that I was lost and gone forever.

I was too afraid to take my own life since I knew if there was a God and a day of judgment, the last thing I wanted was to meet Him and have to account for my actions. I felt like the fire and brimstone mentioned in the scriptures was burning me up in my mind. I wondered if there was such a thing as just ceasing to exist, but I realized that wasn't an option that was in my power to make happen.

Even as I thought I was a damned soul, I concluded that it wouldn't hurt to try to turn my life around even though I had little belief or hope that I could do it. So that is what I did. I didn't wish I was somewhere else—I determined I had to start from where I was and go from there. It seemed that the minute I turned my face toward the light, something inside me was like a war. There were opposing sides, one saying it was too late and I had lost my soul and the other saying if I would put forth the effort I could still be forgiven. That was more than a figurative war in my mind. It was like being torn between two huge powerful forces, and I was the one who had to side with one or the other and that would make the difference.

I decided to go with the light. Shutting out the dark voice was not easy. At the most inappropriate times those dark thoughts would creep back into my mind. It seemed that the only thing that would chase them away was if I would keep looking toward the Light.

Then I experienced something that changed my life and might help others do the same. Every time I would slip backwards, the dark voice loudly accused me and assured me that my efforts to reform were fruitless. However, as long as I continued to face the Light and try again, my horrible past didn't return. It was only if I gave up and consciously turned my back again against the Light that my dark past had the power to drag me down and destroy the hope I had for reformation.

Even when I made some rather serious mistakes (which I did on multiple occasions), if my face was still looking toward the Light, the shadowy past was still behind me. And I discovered something else. The harder I tried to identify and rid myself of those things I knew were offensive to God, the more I sensed His help in picking me up and helping me to get back on the strait and narrow path leading back to His presence. He didn't expect me to do it by myself. He was willing and very able to supplement my weaknesses, giving me power I didn't know I had—actually I didn't have the necessary power on my own. He offered His grace, which I learned was divine enabling power, and that was more than sufficient to repel the darkness that seemed to never give up in trying to drag me back and destroy me.

Eventually I thought I could see a light at the end of the tunnel of darkness that I had travelled in for so long. I hadn't realized that the Light had been there all the time. It was the direction I was facing that prevented me from seeing the Light. The closer I came, the more I recognized that the light at the end of the tunnel was the Light of the World—Christ. He and He alone had the power and the knowhow I needed to free myself from the hell I had created for myself.

How I wish I had never taken that soul-destroying detour. It cost me my wife and family, my life, my self-esteem, almost my very soul. But I can't go back and undo that. I have noticed, however, that the progress I missed out on can be overcome by the speed at which I am improving now.

I can see so many people travelling that same course that I took. I just want to scream at them and warn them that they are speedily approaching the rapids that will lead to their eternal destruction. Unfortunately, like myself, too few are willing to pause long enough to project where they will end up if they continue the course they are pursuing. However, I have hope that at that same "point of no return" that I arrived at, many, if not all of them, will realize that with the help of the Light of the World, they can recover, rid themselves from that all-consuming black hole, and climb back onto the path that brings them the happiness they are seeking and a hope that eventually there will be an eternal reward awaiting them when earth life is over.

I have pondered for years Joe's insight about turning his back on the Light and facing the darkness. More particularly, his observation that even if he slipped and fell as long as he was still facing the Light his dark past did not return to engulf and destroy him. I still marvel how a loving, personal God can tolerate our slipping and sliding and still immediately reach out to us as we turn toward Him. How can he know exactly what we need, when we need it, and how to give it to us with so many billions of people on the earth? I don't know the answer to that other than to say that I know He knows and does all in His limitless power to help every son or daughter back to His presence—not forcing us but willingly helping us when we allow Him.

POINTS TO PONDER

- Have you or someone you care about ever hit rock bottom and felt there was no way out?
- How have you found the strength to carry on?
- Could your quest to regain control of your life have been expedited if you had turned to God sooner?
- How would you try to help someone you love who has lost hope regain the desire to carry on and move forward?

13

WHEN I KNOW I'M GOING TO DIE

From Concern to Comfort

It happens to everyone sooner or later. However, when a doctor explains that you have a terminal disease and no cure is available, the reactions vary. Such was the case with Lynn. He had always been the picture of health, always on the move, and ever ready to help others. He was a handyman's handyman. On a regular physical exam and with further testing, it was determined that he had cancer. Treatment slowed the progress of the disease but did not cure him. As the years passed, the disease progressed. His doctor's visits were more frequent with predictable projections on how long he had to live growing shorter with each visit.

Lynn's story is not unique. Sooner or later we'll all face that uncertain door. My first exposure to death was when my father passed away at age thirty-three; I was four and a half years old. It seems that death has been a rather constant companion over the years. There seems to be at least three different reactions to the impending death.

Lynn typifies the first. He seems at peace with the prospects. He is still relatively young by today's standard. At sixty-seven he had anticipated many more years to spend with his family, pursuing hobbies, and enjoying life. When I asked how he viewed his death, he said that he had no fear but wondered what it would be like and what comes afterward. He is a firm believer in God and seems to trust Him explicitly.

Gary is a different case. A lifetime of drinking and playing in the fast lane has resulted in a body that has recently developed multiple ominous symptoms. He has not focused his life on God or an afterlife, so he is approaching his predicted death with a degree of fear. Many of the questions he asked me centered around my understanding of a life after death. For him death looms as the ultimate mystery door. He has seen others of his drinking buddies pass away and wonders what their receptions have been on the other side of death.

I asked him if he had considered turning to God in these final months of his life. He said that he figured that would be hypocritical and really wouldn't do any good. His increasingly frequent visits to the doctor each time he felt a new pain was diagnosed by the hospital's social worker as a frequent practice of people who have things in their lives of a spiritual nature that are not resolved. When Gary told me what the social worker said, I suggested he at least give it a try to turn to God and see what happened. Although he was skeptical at first, he started praying. Our conversations focused more and more on the feelings he was experiencing. He didn't say he was bubbling over with the Spirit, but he said it was like there was a light on the inside of him that made him feel peaceful.

Slowly, but perceivably, faith in God began to replace the fear of dying. Just before Gary passed away, he lamented that he wished he had turned toward God a lot sooner. He said he had a truckload of regrets but realized he couldn't change that now. He expressed that he was developing some hope that in the next life (which he said he now fully believed in) he could make some amends to his family and friends for letting them down and possibly even do something that would be smiled on favorably by God.

The one thing that I noted over those final months was Gary's countenance. He seemed to go from a more sullen, fearful man to one who smiled and seemed more at ease with himself. His wife and children all said the same thing. We were all left with the question: "Is it ever too late to turn toward God and feel His approving smile no matter how far or how long we have wandered?" My conclusion, based on dozens of similar experiences, is that it is never too late. It certainly won't hurt—you have nothing to lose.

The third approach to death has more to do with those who are left behind. Accidents or suicide leave no time for the family and loved ones to prepare. Although accidental deaths are often very painful, they are not always the fault of the deceased. The thoughtless actions of others often inflict untold pain on the innocent family members.

The more difficult death for survivors or family members is when one takes his or her own life. So many questions are left unanswered. Could the family have intervened and prevented this from happening? Were there undetected warning signs? Was someone else to blame? Did the person feel bullied, abandoned, teased, and so on? Had some unwise decisions of the deceased resulted from activities on the internet? Had someone on social media taunted them into taking their life? The questions seem endless, but the net result is still same—a loved one is gone.

As Gary found some peace and understanding as he turned to God before his death, so the family and friends can find a degree of peace by turning to the same Source. The philosophies of the world (that exclude God) hold very little comfort in those hyper-emotional times.

Whether a family is religious or not, it will do no harm to consult a priest, minister, or person of faith. They may not have all of the answers—none of us do—but they may have more insights and a stronger faith than we do, which in turn gives us hope that we may not have had.

While it is true that we don't know exactly what the next life holds, with increasing faith in a loving, personally involved God, we gain some consolation that even the loved one who has taken his own life may not have totally destroyed the possibility of a bright, glorious future. It is always wise, in cases such as these, to leave judgment alone with God.

We will never know, in this life, what was going on in the life and mind of the loved one who took his own life. Perhaps when we see from the next life all of the conditions that lead up to the act, we will be satisfied that he did as well as could be expected given the opposition he was facing in life.

The loved ones of those who died as a result of accidents say things such as, "Why did this happen to them? Why didn't God intervene and save them? It seems so unfair for God to allow young parents to be killed and leave their children orphans." The questions are endless, but the answers are incomplete or totally absent.

The death of my father when I was so young caused me to ask those questions and many more. However, having lived a long time, it has become apparent that what I considered a tragedy really has been for my benefit. I suspect when we stand with God in the next life and review all of the twists and turns our lives on earth took, we will be constrained to admit that everything worked out for our good and the benefit of everyone associated with us. I realize that takes a huge leap of faith to accept, but what are your options? You can become angry at God, which so many do, and turn your back on Him. What will you put in place of your abandoned faith? Then, what if you discover, after you have died, that God really was there for you and trying (without overcoming your agency) to make things right for you and you refused to look to Him for comfort and understanding?

I am confident that God has a plan for each of His spirit children on earth. If we continue to look to Him, everything will work out not only for those who die, but also for those who are temporarily left behind. Look to God and get the help He offers when death deprives us of continued association with our loved ones. The separation will be temporary. God promises that!

POINTS TO PONDER

- Sooner or later we will all face that uncertain door called death. Have you thought about your final hour in mortality?
- What would you say to your family and loved ones?
- Are there regrets that can be avoided if you make changes now?
- How would you comfort the family of one who has taken his or her own life?
- Have you considered how long you should prolong your life if the prognosis for a quality life is not very good?
- Have you thought about what will happen after death?

14

WHERE DO I GET MY SELF-WORTH?

From Worldliness to Worth

Who am I really? In the eyes of others, my worth seems to be inextricably tied to how much money I make, what kind of car I drive, and the size and location of my home. This is what Frank said as he sat on a park bench, seemingly in the depths of despair:

I grew up in a family that was very socially conscious. The clothes we wore had to be the kind that let people know we had money. I never rode to school in a bus. Either my parents drove me to school, or in high school, I had my own car. It was sort of ingrained in me to believe that my total worth was something people could see, account on a ledger sheet, or hear about.

After graduating from college, I got a job with a prestigious company that paid me a great salary and gave me the opportunity to move up in the company. Over the years I accumulated an amazing number of "things"—a boat, an RV, a motorcycle, and an airplane, to name a few. Life was good. Unwisely, I followed the philosophy of the world and bought as much as I could on credit. My home was mortgaged to the max. I had outstanding debts on all of the toys I owned.

Then came the unhappy day when my fantasy world collapsed. The economy took a downturn, which resulted into the downsizing of the company. The president concluded that middle management (where I was) had to be economized. I was let go. With no means of income and the job market very competitive, and my required salary beyond that of many other people qualified for the job I was seeking, my job searches always came up empty.

Before long the creditors were demanding payment. I sold off as many of my toys as I could to meet my obligations. Before long everything I could liquidate had been sold. The last thing to go was my house. Well, I guess that was the second to last thing. The last thing was my wife. She stayed as long as she could, but sensing the futility of our situation she decided to look for greener pastures—which weren't difficult to find considering the barren desert I found myself in.

There was only one thing left to do to find some relief from the ever-present bill collectors—declare bankruptcy. That was a personally devastating day since from my earliest days I had equated my self-worth with the money I earned and the things I owned. Now I had nothing but the clothes on my back and no place to turn.

In that darkest of all days, on a park bench in the midst of despair I cried out to God—something I hadn't done in years. I didn't expect, nor did I receive, a vision or a voice confirming that He was there and heard me. But I did experience a calm that I cannot explain. It wasn't like things would get better and I would be rich again. It was more like, "I am aware of your condition. I will not abandon you like you have abandoned me. Just evaluate where you are, take stock of your assets, and I'll help you get pointed in the right direction." It was the strangest sensation I have ever had. I even looked around to see if someone was whispering to me. No one was there.

I felt total frustration because I didn't know where to start from where I was. The thoughts I had had were undeniable, but they didn't tell me what to do. I sat back on the bench and tried to take stock of what assets I had. I didn't have much. Then it dawned on me that I had my health and a willingness to work. I decided I couldn't just walk into some company and demand the salary comparable to what I was making before I was laid off.

It took eating some humble pie, but I applied for a job at a fast food place. They hired me, but they knew and I knew that I was cut out for something far greater than flipping hamburgers. Dutifully, I showed up early for each of my shifts. I actually became pretty good at flipping hamburgers and serving drinks. Before long I was promoted to shift manager. It was still something I knew I didn't want to make a lifelong career. My managerial talents were put to good use, and soon the employees under my supervision began to respond to my leadership style. I guess I had more resources than I originally thought.

Almost a year later, I was invited to interview for a position in the corporate office. They noted my dependability, my punctuality, my work ethic, and my ability to work with people. I was sort of taken aback because I thought those were things that just went along with the job. I got the job and a huge pay raise.

I was much more cautious how I used my funds. I didn't need the designer clothes. My car didn't need to be the newest and most expensive model on the road. My apartment was modest but adequate. I had no room to store the toys I had surrounded myself with before I was laid off. Consequently I was very deliberate in what I purchased.

Now it has been fifteen years since that day I thought my world had come to an end. I have just been promoted to executive vice-president of the company. Along the way I remarried, and we've started our family. My children question why I am so strict about them having to earn their own way, buy their own clothes, and take responsibility for their own actions. It has become clear to me that to give someone everything without any responsibility to take accountability for their own actions is not a wise thing to do.

Would I wish what happened to me on anyone else? My initial answer would be no. But on second thought, the lessons I have learned, my necessity to reconnect and rely upon God, and then to listen for and recognize His promptings are worth all the ease and luxury the world can afford. In fact, the lie the world seems to be drinking to their destruction is that the world owes everyone a living. This entitlement attitude I see escalating around us and infiltrating our political institutions is a danger we want to avoid.

When someone thinks that the world owes them a living and they just sit around waiting for someone to do something for them, they are setting themselves up for frustration and disappointment. On the other hand, if you expect nothing and someone does something for you, a sense of gratitude wells up inside you. The trite saying that we should develop the "attitude of gratitude" has a more far-reaching application than we sometimes see. It can and should permeate every aspect of our lives.

I hope this hasn't been too preachy, but if my experience is typical, the key to success in life isn't in the things we can accumulate or the positions we hold, or the money we have in the bank. The real success in life is the good we can do for others in helping them achieve their potential, in leaving the world a better place than you found it, and in partnering with God in helping others turn to Him for help in meeting life's challenges.

Frank is not unique in either his attitude about what constitutes success or in his eventually realizing how empty and hollow the world's definition of success is. Unfortunately, I have seen many people who have gone to their graves still trying to find the illusive happiness that money, prestige, and notoriety promises bring.

POINTS TO PONDER

- What would do if your world collapsed around you tomorrow?
- Where would you start to rebuild your life?
- Are you investing wisely?
- If the economy tanked next week, are you positioned to survive?
- What steps could you take now to prepare for an uncertain future?
- Do you have loved ones who could benefit from your counsel?
- Would a reevaluation of your life's priorities have eternal benefits?
- Could you reach out to others and help them do that same midcourse evaluation?

15

ESCAPING DRUDGERY OR DESTROYING LIFE

From Mistakes to Finding Meaning

Life for many stay-at-home moms can become a drudgery. It doesn't have to be, but in today's world having a career for women is the ultimate success. For those who are visionary enough to see that what they do in molding the rising generation far exceeds any worldly honor and accomplishment, they need to recognize their contribution but be aware of the potential pitfalls.

Janis is one who came close to destroying everything she had worked so hard to build. Here is her story as she recounted it to me:

I was a happily married wife and mother of four little children. We had a great marriage, and I loved spending time with my children. After a number of years, our children were all in school and I had time on my hands. I had a college degree and my husband and I considered my entering the workforce. We concluded that it was more important that I be there when the children came home from school or activities. It is too obvious the impact that the breakdown in the family is causing worldwide.

Then the answer to the question of what to do productively with my time became an urgent need. I started to "surf the net" to see what others were doing. Then I joined the billions on Facebook. Soon I had a

Twitter account and became fairly proficient with Instagram. It didn't take long before I was reconnecting with friends from high school and other places where we had lived. It was so satisfying to see what everyone was doing. Then I started to get more and more friend requests from people I did not know but who were were friends with some of my friends.

Before long I was spending multiple hours each day keeping in touch. Then I starting Facebooking with a friend of a friend. He was a guy that seemed to have very similar interests as I had. It was just a comfortable sharing friendship. However, without realizing what was happening, I started to develop feelings deeper than mere friendship with him. I knew it was wrong, but with my husband being so busy at work and the kids away at school, it seemed natural to share our feelings of lack of fulfillment.

It was a sorry day when we expressed to each other the feelings we were having for each other. We both knew nothing would ever come of it, but rather than cut it off immediately, we continued our private relationship. In retrospect I can't begin to tell you what allowed me to get trapped into sexting with him. At first, we were just exchanging photos. Then, at his suggestion, I sent him a photo that was somewhat more revealing. He praised the way I looked—something my husband hadn't done for some time. Then came the day that he asked me to send him a revealing photo. At first I declined, knowing that once the photo was sent, I could never get it back.

Giving into his pleadings to share and his continuing to praise my physical beauty, I finally sent him a semi-nude picture. He was ecstatic. He continued to pressure me for a full-frontal nude photo. I resisted for some time and finally sent him one. Then things changed. He started to suggest that unless I met him for sex, he would post the photos on the internet and it would ruin my marriage, my family, and my whole life.

At this point I finally had a reality check. I had been dubbed and could see no way out. Thank God I refused to meet him. He continued to hound me, but I stopped Facebooking with him. Knowing that he could ruin my life, I confessed to my husband, who was devastated but willing to work it through with me. He answered one of the Facebook messages the guy sent to me, threatening to take legal action against him if he ever posted a picture of me. To this point in time, nothing has been posted on the internet, but I live in constant fear that he will figure some way of posting the picture under a fake name.

It has taken some time to regain the trust of my husband. To this point none of our children are aware of what happened. It was foolish, and I regret ever being so stupid as to fall for the trick. But that innocent part of life I squandered away for a thrill robbed me of the ability to hold my head high no matter where I go in society.

Since my horrible experience I have become aware of the number of similar experiences women have had. In one case an acquaintance who lived not far from me got involved in an internet romance. She ended up abandoning her husband and children and moving in with her internet lover. She was sure she had made a good choice until her husband started dating another woman. She was enjoying the sleazy dresses, the drunken parties, the dazzling life the world glorifies.

Then she realized that she really loved her husband and children. When her husband proposed to his new girlfriend (the divorce having been final for a couple of years), my acquaintance came to him and begged him to take her back. Her children, now teenagers, had pleaded with their mother not to go with the other guy. She was sure she was doing the right thing. Now her children, when asked by their father if they would accept her back as their mother, said they would prefer his new girlfriend who is an outstanding woman.

It was a very sad day when the husband married the new wife and the old wife was invited not to interfere in the lives of her children. Some mistakes, like the one Janis made, can be overcome. Other mistakes, like the one just described, have consequences that have lasting effects.

The internet can be such a blessing and a powerful tool. However, unless you control it and make it serve you, it can become a soul-destroying monster. If you never allow yourself to visit sites you know are destructive, you will never become addicted. If you control the time you spend surfing the net or joining chat groups or reconnecting with old friends, you can benefit greatly and your life can be richer. However, there is a flip side of that coin. If you lose control in any of those areas, the cry is to stop where you are, get control, set the rules, and proceed cautiously.

To the women or men who have started down that slippery path, wouldn't it be wise to take a huge step back and consider where you might end up if you continue on that path? For those who realize that they have already made serious mistakes either on what they have disclosed or the relationships they have started to establish, retreat immediately and avoid the devastation described above. Know that you can regain control of your situation even if it is painful. With the help of God, all of us can start over again or, better, avoid the illusionary vision the world portrays as the way of happiness.

POINTS TO PONDER

- Everyone makes mistakes—not always life-destroying ones but mistakes that head our lives in a direction we don't want to go. Have you made those kinds of "detours"? How have you corrected them?
- Would recognizing the problem earlier have made recovery easier?
- What stands in the way of your regaining control of your life?
- Can you help others who feel they have lost their opportunity for a quality life regain that hope?
- Are there areas you know you will have to correct before you can enjoy total happiness?

16

NOWHERE TO TURN

From Skepticism to Spirituality

Derek is one of the nicest guys I have ever met. He is a retired engineer, a husband, a father, a true friend, and an atheist. His is one of the most interesting stories I have included in this book. We met while my wife and I were on a Caribbean cruise. For five days we shared ideas concerning different aspects of our views on life. This is a synopsis of Derek's story:

Derek grew up a church-going Christian. From his youth through adolescence, he attended church meetings with his family and friends. However, life had its twists and turns. As Derek sought understanding to the more perplexing questions, he found that the church's doctrine didn't satisfy his inquiring mind. The fulfillment he expected to find in religious involvement was mostly absent. What fulfillment there was he attributed to social interactions with his friends.

Derek began to look for empirical evidence that proved there was a God. He found none! One of his fellow engineers introduced him to a book by a prominent atheist. According to Derek's account, he devoured the book and found explanations that satisfied his most basic questions. He accepted that there were moral ways of interacting with humankind but that there were no absolute right or wrongs.

As he expected, his family and religious friends were appalled at his abandonment of traditional Christian beliefs. He had many long and heated debates where he challenged their beliefs and asked for verifiable evidence of the existence of God. Since religion is based on faith in an unseen being, and given his talent to articulate his atheistic philosophy, Derek often felt victorious at the end of the debates.

Over time his family stopped challenging him, and many of his friends distanced themselves from him. New friends who ascribed to his atheistic philosophy replaced the old friends. His continued studies in atheistic philosophy only confirmed what he believed to be true. Once he had finished his formal education, Derek found a position with a large engineering firm. Although many of his fellow engineers were staunch Christians, they seldom discussed his atheistic beliefs. When religion did come up, he found ample opportunities to share his ever-growing atheistic philosophy. According to his account, those discussions were often met with stiff resistance from those who held a strong belief in God. They were more articulate than his family and former friends had been and so were not as easily intimidated.

Life moved on. Derek married and had children. They seemed to be comfortably suited to living a happy life. Although not an atheist, his wife fashioned herself as an agnostic—neither accepting God nor denying that He existed but claiming that even if God does exist, He has nothing to do with humankind. Derek's family relationship had improved, especially with his siblings. They accepted him for who he was. He had an especially loving relationship with his nieces and nephews.

Then the tragedy struck. His favorite nephew in his last year of graduate school took his own life. With no belief in a life following this one, Derek was devastated. It was in this condition that we met for our five-day exchange of ideas about religion and life. During the arranged meetings while at sea and during dinners in which we agreed to meet, we explored our differences about our personal beliefs.

Derek explained his unresolvable dilemma. He had no belief in a life following death, but he had an unquenchable desire to see his nephew again. I offered my strong belief that the spirit of his departed nephew was alive and well in a world or condition not far from us and that he would one day receive his body again as a resurrected being. These concepts were not totally foreign to Derek given his youth and adolescence while attending church. He said he wished he could believe that but just couldn't bring himself to believe in such a remarkable possibility. It was a "leap of faith" that his scientific mind just couldn't make.

For a good part of the five-day cruise, we talked about Derek's nephew, the purpose of life, the existence of God, the plan that God has for His spirit children, and what one has to do to gain that knowledge for himself. Derek met all of this with skepticism. There was no attempt on my part to impose my beliefs on Derek. It was simply an honest, intellectual exchange of ideas. But the amount of information shared and the testimony expressed left little doubt that I was a firm believer in God.

I didn't hear from Derek again for some years. My attempts to keep up with him went unanswered. Then one day I got a letter. In his letter he explained that he had dismissed our previous conversations as fables and returned to his former position following the cruise. However, according to his account, the reflections of those conversations continued to haunt him. What if what we had discussed was true? What if his beloved nephew really was alive in a spirit world? What if the near-impossible concept of a literal resurrection and a continuation of life into an eternal world was really true?

In one of his more ponderous times, he had taken a trip alone to his cabin near a lake. He said as he sat staring at the beauties of nature around him, he began to wonder if all of this could have happened by chance. He said he sat there long into the evening. As the sun set and darkness crept in, he saw the stars as they began to appear. As he looked heavenward, the beauty and magnificence and order of the universe nearly overwhelmed him. Again, he pondered whether all that could possibly have happened by chance. He said he had, in that singular setting, gone from wondering about the microscopic to the macroscopic worlds around him.

He didn't see God or hear a voice, but he saw fingerprints of a super intelligence creating and directing the worlds around him. At that time, he did not admit to believing in God, but he did say that the evidence supporting a Divine Power being the creator rather than some evolutionary explanation seemed more plausible. Then he made what I consider an astute observation. He said, "It all depends on what you are looking for. I have looked for an explanation apart from God as the answer to what I see around me. I thought I saw it. Then I started looking for evidence of a Divine Creator and virtually everything I saw seemed to verify that there is a God. Everything from the microscopic world of electrons, protons, and atoms to the macroscopic stars, galaxies, and universes discovered by the Hubble telescope. To think that all this happened by chance, by a big bang, required a larger stretch of faith than believing that a Divine Being using unlimited power caused these things to happen."

He concluded that he was struggling to accept by faith what was abundantly evident by viewing the things around him. I wrote back assuring him of the existence of a Higher Power. I encouraged him to lay aside his skepticism and humbly pray to God for some kind of a witness that God really does exist and that He knows Derek and all people on earth and is not an absentee God but a loving, kind Heavenly Father who is vitally interested in all people and is anxiously awaiting an invitation to be involved in the very details of each person's life.

Although the lines of communication have gone silent again, I am confident if Derek will humbly look upward, he will get the testimony that transcends sight. He will come to know for himself that God really does exist and that this life is merely a preparatory experience readying us for a never-ending life to come.

Perhaps atheism is the most difficult challenge to overcome because it moves the person from one end of the spectrum to the other. However, when that move takes place, the rewards are also the greatest. Feelings never before experienced are awaiting him or her. Mind-expanding insights will come. From the experience of other former atheists I have encountered, the mental visions they attest have happened to them dispelled forever the indescribably dark confining influences of philosophies designed to explain the wonders of nature around us by excluding a belief in God.

So, to those who are still under the influence of atheism, why not take a chance? Look upward and see if that same transformation that is happening to Derek will happen to you. If it does (and I'm confident it will!) your view of life will forever change. It is worth the effort to find out for yourself.

POINTS TO PONDER

- Is your world view affording you the happiness and security you desire?
- Have you taken the time to ponder the end of your life if you continue the direction you are going?
- Have you considered the "theocentric" or God-centered life and what promises it makes to the faithful?

- Are you tolerant of those who disagree with your philosophy?
- Have you spent time trying to understand where others are coming from?
- Are you open to intellectual exchange where others differ from you?
- Have you ever or are you willing to take that leap of faith and consider the existence of God?

17

LIVING LIFE UNDER A CLOUD

From Depression to Devotion

The purpose of this vignette is not to suggest that depression is not a real thing or that those so afflicted can, with effort, overcome it. I am not dealing with clinical depression that has a physiological cause. However, what I learned from working with people suffering from depression may be of help. It certainly will not hurt to give it a try. Anything is better than living under a cloud of depressing darkness. Depression robs the person of so many of the joys and happiness of life, it looks like there should be some divine help in controlling it.

Nick is the composite story of those who have done all in their power to control their depressive feelings. According to Nick's account, the first step was to realize what he was experiencing. Denying that he was depressed only postponed the time when he could take control. He said: "Darkness feeds on itself." The more he told himself he was depressed, the deeper into depression he went. His experience with anti-depressants was not positive. He said that too often following his medication he would have episodes of increased depression and even feelings of suicide. In listening to the advertisements on television, they seem to issue the same warnings. That doesn't mean that some people (maybe many) respond positively to medications. But for those who do not and those who want to try something in addition to medication, perhaps some of the following suggestions can help.

Each person with depression I have talked to said that turning to God for help was a huge first step. Each had to avoid the temptation of blaming God for their condition. Doing so only seemed to add to the frustration and deepening depression rather than helping them overcome and control it. One of the commonly reported effects of turning to God for help was that their struggles with depression took on an air of a challenge rather than some divine punishment.

Nick said he started to view his struggle with depression as an opportunity to develop strengths that he didn't realize he had. With his turning to God, Nick also began to pray for help. Expecting divine help gave him courage to try a little harder and persevere a little longer, and resist falling into a feeling of despair because he realized that with God all things are possible. Next Nick said he tried (better when he wasn't as depressed) to identify what he called triggers. What experiences, places, people, diets, and so on seemed to set off his depressive episodes? He said the sooner he could identify his descent into the darkness of depression, the easier it was to take actions to counteract the decline. He emphasized that early recognition, not denial, was crucial in taking control.

Nick was pretty definite in suggesting that what works for one person may not always work for others. Sometimes, what previously had worked for him didn't have the same impact the next time. Therefore, he suggested having a list of things that could act as antidotes to control the depressive spirit. When I queried what some of the things on his list were, he said praying, physical exercise, calling a friend to go do some activity or just to talk, reading a good book, or watching a television show that was funny and somewhat mindless. He said reading scriptures or a good book helped. He suggested talking to a counselor, priest, or minister. For him, indulging in a favorite meal or dessert seemed to increase his blood sugar and give him more determination to beat the monster. And even though physical exercise was not his "go to" activity, it did help to go for a jog or run.

I could tell that Nick had given some serious thought to his life of nonmedical anti-depressants. He laughingly assured me that others could add to his list with little effort, but some serious introspective thought was a must for each person wanting to control his depression. Then he changed directions on me. He said that there were certain things he absolutely needed to avoid. Some of those were listed as triggers, but some fell into his strategies for controlling the depression. At the top of his list was "avoid *all* negative self-talk." He discovered that whenever he told himself that he was depressed, it became a self-fulfilling prophecy. The moment he found himself allowing negative, dark thoughts into his mind, he immediately went to his list of anti-depressant antidotes noted above. He admitted that at times he almost felt like he had earned the right to be depressed. That, however, was a downward spiral that never had a good ending. He avoided people who sympathized with his struggle and would say things like, "Poor Nick, I feel your pain. I wish I could trade places with you for a few minutes while you got some relief." That kind of help, although sincerely offered, was the opposite of what he needed. Maybe some others need that kind of reinforcement, but he didn't. He learned that certain people seemed to make it more difficult to control his feelings. It wasn't that they were necessarily bad people; it was just that he realized the influence they had on him made it harder to stay positive. Maybe someday he will be able to strengthen himself so he can re-engage with them without becoming depressed.

Nick said he had identified a person who was bubbly and could carry both sides of a conversation with little or no input from him. He would call her just to chat, knowing that forty-five minutes later with him saying little or nothing, he would hang up feeling like a whirlwind had taken him to a new height.

He identified what at first glance appeared to be a contradiction. He said sometimes he needed to be around people and sometimes he needed to be alone without any outside distractions. Since those battling depression often withdraw from social situations, I wondered if he wasn't playing into the hands of the depression. However, on closer consideration, I could see that at times the depressed person needed some space to gather their resources so they could rejoin the battle. It was sort of like a "time-out" in sports. Just a brief time to catch one's breath before continuing the fight.

Many of the people I have talked with over the years have developed strategies that have worked for them. Others, in despair, have resigned themselves to a life living under the cloud. I haven't found anyone who got up in the morning hoping to be depressed that day. All of them wanted to be happy and enjoy life. Those who used any and all resources to control the monster depression always fared better than those who sat passively by and waited for someone to do something for them.

Calling upon the Lord for whatever help He chooses to give works best when we are constantly aware of any help that may be available. Nick and others often said that God had really helped them, but it was usually through some other person that their prayers were answered.

If depression is one of the challenges life affords you, why not look toward God, identify the triggers, devise multiple positive plans, list the negatives, and then go to with your might having full confidence that God is aware of you and will never require more of you than you are capable of doing? Remember what Paul, the ancient apostle, said to the church members in Corinth: "There hath no temptation taken you but such as is common to man: but God *is* faithful, who will not suffer you to be tempted above that ye are able; but will with the temptation also make a way to escape, that ye may be able to bear it" (1 Corinthians 10:13).

Armed with the confidence that God never tells a lie, look for "the escape" He has promised from this monster and all other challenges you are facing.

POINTS TO PONDER

- Are you open to suggestions on how to cope with depressive feelings?
- Are you critical of those who suffer from debilitating depression?
- Have you sought profession help to gain coping strategies that may lessen the impact of your depression?
- Have you lost hope of ever recovering?
- Have you sought help through prayer, scripture reading, and talking to a priest or minister?
- Have you ever looked at your struggles as opportunities to develop character strengths?
- Are you willing to patiently carry on when relief does not come immediately?
- Have you avoided the fruitless anger and blaming God for your condition?

18

CORRUPTION IN THE CHURCH

From Disappointing Dependence to Determined Independence

One of the most faith-destroying trials that seems to be happening with increased frequency is the revelation of corruption by ministers and priests. People in positions of trust in the churches engaging in behavior that is diametrically opposite from what they preach is heartbreaking to every believer. If one's faith is founded in the men and women who officiate in the church, core beliefs may be shattered when they see the corruption that exists in the church—not necessarily in the church itself, but in those entrusted to officiate in the church. This was the case with Jeremy. Here is his story:

I had always looked at church as God's place of refuge from the world. I viewed those in positions of trust as being near-perfect. For years as a child and on into adulthood, I believed that every leader in the church was someone I could trust and pattern my life after. You can imagine the feelings of devastation I felt when several members of our congregation accused the priest of sexually abusing them.

My first reaction was to question the honesty of the accusers. How could they possibly come up with such incredible lies considering the position and years of selfless service the priest had given? It wasn't until a formal charge was issued against him that I began to look at the facts. I knew the accusers. They were good, honorable women. What motive could they have to make up the stories of abuse?

Then my questioning mind began to expand the accusations. What if the doctrine and teachings of the church were also just made up? Not so slowly my faith was shattered. I quit attending church. I was totally disillusioned with the whole concept of a personal God who spoke to men through prophets in old times and what they had written as scriptures. What if they were no more than ancient traditions? A very real darkness seemed to envelop me from head to toe. I lost my zest for life and felt totally lost with virtually nowhere to turn.

Then the process of trying to make sense out of life began in earnest. If not God, then what? If I was going to abandon God, what did I have to take His place? The very purpose of life came into question. If the commandments that God had revealed for our happiness and safety were just ancient fables, what basis did I have for determining right and wrong? Is whatever one thinks right in his own eyes okay? What if what one person thinks is all right is in direct opposition to what other people say is okay? The questions seemed to be endless.

It didn't take long before I felt like I was swimming in a whirlpool that had no bottom and no way out. The whole of my life, and apparently the lives of everyone else I knew, centered around the Judeo-Christian God and His commandments. I tried to figure out the logic behind the commandments. Each time I came to a conclusion, I could see the wisdom behind the commandments. I should have engaged in that kind of exercise years before rather than just accepting everything that the priest said as the infallible truth.

As I expanded the scope of my search, I determine that God really didn't have anyone else to do His work other than imperfect men and women. As far as I could tell from reading the Bible, there was only One person who had ever lived a perfect life. So, to base my judgment on the perfect behavior of leaders in the church was a huge mistake. After all, the ancient Apostle Peter had denied Christ three times but was still designated by Christ as the leader of His church after His resurrection and ascension.

Then I began what turned out to be a very fruitful venture—separating the rightness or wrongness of a teaching from those entrusted to administer and teach the principle. I think that all started as I turned my judgmental eye inward. To my surprise, I realized that while I demanded perfection from others, I was more than willing to excuse my own weaknesses. I didn't pretend to be perfect, so I avoided labeling myself as a hypocrite. However, my scathing condemnation of others seemed not to apply directly to myself.

One day a close friend noticed my absence from church services. In a sometimes-heated discussion, he pointed out the dual standard I seemed to have adopted—it was okay for me to be imperfect, but I didn't want to extend that same liberty to others. I think I was too proud to admit that during the discussion, but later that night I lay awake pondering what he had said. He was right, of course. I really was being hypocritical.

As a parting shot, before ending the debate, he asked me to consider the level of enjoyment in my life since I had distanced myself from God. I pondered that question late into the night. Being totally honest with myself, I had to admit that life didn't hold the same level of happiness and excitement as when I was fully engaged in using the commandments to meet the challenges of life. Without God, there wasn't a purpose for life. Without God's plan for mankind, there wasn't direction to avoid unhappiness and see life as a series of tests to improve ourselves. Without a well-defined gospel, there was no litmus test to determine whether I was on the path leading back to God.

Now I had the self-imposed task of determining how to be content in an imperfect church, administered by imperfect people, and still not lose my faith in a perfect God, His perfect plan, and His willingness to tutor me in spite of my individual weaknesses. First, I had to conclude that God really did exist. Next, I had to admit that His commandments were perfect and applicable in my life. Then I had to stop tying my beliefs to the actions of fallible men and women—myself being one of them! Finally, I had to make the faith-based leap that Jesus really is the Son of God who has atoned for my sins and has shown by the life He lived how to return to the presence of God.

I must admit that some of those steps were easier than others. I had always believed in God and Christ—that wasn't so difficult to re-establish. Separating people from their actions was much more difficult. How could I possibly look at a person who was sinning and not condemn him? I thought of Christ and the woman taken in adultery (see John 8:1–11). He said that He didn't condemn her at that time but charged her to go and sin no more. Couldn't I do the same? Christ obviously did not condone or approve of the adultery, but He saw the value of the adulteress apart from the act.

Finally, I realized that if I was really a committed Christian, I had to give more than a token effort to keep the commandments and live a Christlike life. I am not anywhere close to being perfect, but with the decisions I made and my focus on personal perfection rather than trying to exercise the role of Christ as the Judge, my life has become much more enjoyable and filled with the Holy Spirit. Do I still wish church leaders would clean up their acts and set a better example? Sure. But now I see that how I live the commandments is infinitely more important than how others live the commandments. Maybe they don't have the same insight I am gaining. But I know that when the Lord said the same standard or measure I use to judge others will be levied against me, I am willing to be patient and tolerable with everyone else.

Jeremy's story has cemented in my mind the concept that my final judgment will be what I have done, not what others have or haven't done. I totally agree with Jeremy. Trying to magnify Christ's role as a judge is not only impossible, but it also requires so much time and energy that I could be using to help others. I guess I'll wait and see if Christ ever asks for my help in passing judgment on mankind. I am confident He never will! Why not join me in refusing to judge others, and enjoy life to the fullest?

POINTS TO PONDER

- Is your faith shaken when clergy stumbles or falls?
- Do you apply the same standard of judgment to your attitude and behavior as you do to those who hold positions of leadership in the church?
- Have you ever tried to console those who have their faith bruised by the actions of others?
- Can you learn from others' mistakes without passing judgment on them?

19

NOTHING CAN STOP YOU

From Wondering Why to Understanding

One area where there is a huge difference in the way people respond is physical handicaps. Some people give up, become bitter, and withdraw into a self-constructed cocoon. Others assess their limitations, make a plan to move ahead, and accomplish amazing things—even when compared with people who have no handicaps.

This story is close to my heart since it deals with a favorite aunt and uncle. Aunt Pat (her real name) was stricken with polio at age fifteen. Uncle Clyde (his real name) contracted polio at eighteen months. Pat was quadriplegic, Clyde was paraplegic. Focusing on both of their remarkable stories would go far beyond the constraints of this book. Pat actually began a book she entitled *Clyde*, which the family asked me to finish following her death.

Part of Pat's story I want to recount dealt with her time in Georgia in an iron lung. Not much hope was extended to her or her companions suffering like illnesses. When the doctors explained to the patients and their parents what lay ahead for them, a number of them literally turned their faces to the wall and died.

Pat was different. She listened carefully to the prognosis, decided she would try to beat the odds, and did everything in her power to prove the doctors wrong. Through years of extensive, exhausting, painful physical therapy, she gained partial use of one hand.

Clyde, on the other hand, never learned to walk. His legs never developed beyond the length and size of an eighteen-month-old. His father made a round board with wheels on the bottom. They called it "the cheese." Clyde became very proficient in maneuvering the cheese. When his friends wanted him to join their fun (which they always did because of his intellect and creativity), they would put him in a wagon or a wheelbarrow, or carry him on their backs.

Considering each of their conditions, it was unlikely that they would experience the normal happenings of life. But over the objections of both families they began to date and eventually married. Learning to live independently required all of the intellect and creativity of both of them.

Clyde eventually became the mayor of the city he lived in. When he could no longer serve because his physical condition declined, Pat took his place. They served until neither could keep the pace required of the one in the mayoral office.

Clyde was a dyed-in-the-wool Democrat, and Pat was a vocal Republican. Both of them were well read in everything from fiction to the classics. It was intellectually stimulating to engage them in deep philosophical discussions. Clyde took the more liberal approach and Pat the conservative role. I joined with Pat on the debates. It was always frustrating when we would get the best of Clyde and he'd just smile and skate off into another room.

Pat was great at helping me with my college papers, especially the one I entitled "The Psychological Effects of a Physical Handicap." It took some time to coerce Pat into admitting that she was an exceptional person. Finally, I succeeded, for the sake of discussion, in getting her to admit she had developed most social skills far beyond others. I took the position she was who she was *because* of her handicap. She argued, on the other hand, that she was who she was *in spite* of her handicap.

From our debate, which lasted over several weeks, we concluded that the handicap didn't determine the person's outcome. The attitude of the handicapped person did. Pat said, "If you think you can or you can't, you are right!" We referenced her friends who had given up when faced with the prospects of life on a lounge or, at best, in a wheelchair.

Our discussions often asked the unanswerable questions such as, why are some people born with handicaps and other are normal? Is God being unfair to those with limited physical or mental capacities? Will people with normal bodies and minds be held to a higher level of accountability on the day of judgment? Why do so many "normal" people function so far below their potential? The questions were endless. The answers caused us both many nights of pondering. Clyde didn't like to join our discussions. He quoted Voltaire, who said: "Things are the way they are supposed to be or they wouldn't be the way they are!" That statement alone caused us to ponder and discuss whether God had a plan for each and every person on earth. The subsequent discussion focused on free will and whether we were predestined to fulfill the role God outlined for us.

From our observations of those around us and people we knew, we concluded that even though God knows the end from the beginning, He allows each of us to make our own choices. How could that be? It worked perfectly well when we decided that God is not on trial—we are. Like a school teacher who knows every answer to every question on a test, God knows what we will do but doesn't cause us to act in any predestined way.

We discussed, ad nauseum, the impact on the individual when everyone dictates what they were and were not capable of doing. Pat was a perfect example. Virtually everyone in her family told her she would never marry or be anything other than a vegetable on a lounge. She refused to accept that label and, through her entire adult life, proved the naysayers wrong. My wife, Vickie, has a saying that is so very true. In counseling a student who had been told all her life that she was stupid (by a step-father), Vickie pointed her finger at the student and with great emphasis said, "Don't you *ever* let anyone define who you are!"

Long after our debates ended, I watched the reaction of people when others tried to dictate, define, or determine who they were and what they could accomplish. Those who acquiesced to the opinions of others never seemed to rise above their designated limits, while those who refused to listen to the opinion of others often rose to great heights.

After many years I took the spotlight and focused the beam on myself. To my surprise I discovered that, at least to a degree, I had allowed others to influence my attitude and behavior. Some were positive comments (my wife being my greatest cheerleader and always telling me I can do anything), others warning me of failure and embarrassment if I pursued some project I had set my sights on. Too often I was overly influenced by the comments of others.

I am not advocating that we tune out everyone who makes suggestions and observations. What I am saying is best expressed in a saying I have adopted and have taught to thousands of students over the years: "Whoever must eventually stand judgment for the decision must be free to make the decision." That sounds like a no-brainer if you analyze it. How would you feel if someone made a decision and you had to suffer the consequences without having any input in the decision?

Many of my college-aged students were contemplating marriage. They wanted anyone other than themselves to decide who they should marry. Mostly they wanted God to tell them who to marry. I would say to them, "Who is going to have to learn to live with your future mate—you or God?" They usually got the answer right, so I would say, "Then you make the decision and let God help you make a successful marriage."

I have come to the conclusion that God is not the One who places ceilings on what we can accomplish—we are. Maybe this would be a good time to erase those self-imposed ceilings and see what you can accomplish. Pat and Clyde have both passed away, but the lessons I learned from them will follow me into the grave. Hopefully the people I have taught over the years will continue their message forever.

POINTS TO PONDER

- Have you ever put "ceilings" on yourself because of the negative comments of others?
- Are you willing to take a chance and put yourself out there when failure is a possibility?
- Have you ever succeeded against the criticism of others?
- Are you able to get back up and try again when you stumble?
- Are you willing to accept responsibility for your actions even when it is hurtful?
- Do you enjoy making decisions as opposed to having others make decisions for you?
- Could anyone in your circle of acquaintances benefit from a pep-talk by you about making decisions?

20

DECEIVED BY ONE I TRUSTED

From Betrayal to Benevolence

There could be any of a hundred names on this scenario. Some of the details might vary, but the hurt, the anger, the feelings of revenge, and the ultimate betrayal are all too common. Although I will use Ned as an example, please understand that this is a combination of dozens of similar experiences with similar feelings and a common solution.

Ned was an optimistic, energetic young college graduate with the world ahead of him. While in college he had developed a close friendship with Bill. Together they had dreamed of starting their own business after graduation and conquering the world. It seemed their world was about to become a reality. Each had married, and most of their social lives revolved around each other.

They had succeeded in convincing a bank to take a chance on them to jumpstart their business. Success was almost immediate. The loan was being repaid, their products were selling, and new items were being added to their offering. The future looked very promising. For several years it seemed they were destined to financial success and a life with all the necessities and many of the luxuries.

Almost without Ned's being aware, they seemed to hit a slump in their profits. As they discussed the problem, they concluded that, like most businesses, they have their ups and downs. They kept working but didn't seem to be realizing the same returns for their efforts. It was a dark and life-changing day when Ned asked an independent auditor to look at their books and discovered that Bill had been stealing from the company for over a year.

How could he do that? If he had only asked, Ned would have loaned him all the money he needed. What had been a close business and personal relationship was shattered in a minute. With the business on the brink of bankruptcy, Bill failed to come to work the next day. Upon investigation, it was discovered that he and his wife had taken their belongings and fled the area. No one knew where they had gone. Ned was left to salvage what he could and rebuild the business, if possible. However, getting Bill's name off the corporate ownership was not easy. According to the law he was still entitled to half of the profits.

The feelings of betrayal, anger, and the desire for revenge grew day by day. Long days, sleepless nights, and struggling to meet financial obligations almost consumed Ned's life. More than anything he wanted the scales of justice to be balanced and Bill to be accountable and make reparations. Ned noticed that his relationship with his wife and children was being strained. All he could talk about at the dinner table and on their date nights was what Bill had done and how difficult the betrayal was.

Ned had always been a religious man and knew that the Bible said he needed to forgive Bill. How could he do that? Bill made no efforts to ask for forgiveness or make things right. It just seemed unreasonable that Ned should have to shoulder not only the business loss but also the mental burden of forgiving. In that state of mind, Ned found himself slipping in a depressive darkness that he had never experienced before. His native optimism had all but disappeared. At the suggestion of his wife, he sought counseling. That didn't seem to help. It looked like the betrayal by his friend and business partner was going to result in his destruction.

In that mental state, Ned turned to a practice he had engaged in for years but had recently abandoned. He started to pray and read the Bible. Sometimes the things he read seemed to condemn him more than offer any hope or help. Matthew 6:15, which says that the Lord will not forgive us if we don't forgive those who wrong us was a hard pill to swallow. There didn't seem to be any fairness or equity in that principle.

During one of those long, sleepless nights, Ned tried to take inventory of the whole messy situation. Like a light penetrating the darkness he realized that he was giving Bill power over him even though he had neither heard from nor seen him since the day he abandoned him. It became apparent that in order for Ned to move ahead, he needed to put the whole matter in the hands of the Lord. But how was he to do that?

The answer didn't come that night, nor for several nights that followed. Then one night the thought came: *I'll let God balance the eternal scales of justice. Let Him judge Bill. Put your trust that God is a just God, and eventually everything will be worked out to your total satisfaction.* As Ned did that, he noticed that it felt like a heavy weight had been lifted from his mind. He could start to see things more clearly and knew what he had to do to repair and rebuild the business. He saw that his relationship with his wife and children had taken a turn toward the positive.

Somehow, which Ned didn't fully realize how, the Lord had lifted his burden. For the first time in months Ned could rest physically at night and mentally during the day. He came to realize that forgiveness wasn't required solely for the benefit of the offender—it was also for the benefit of the offended!

When does that relief come? That seems to depend on the offended. The longer feelings of revenge predominate the mind of the offended, the blessed relief does not come. Of the many people I have interacted with over five decades, it seems that some offended ones have to struggle and take a long time to let the betrayal go. Others seems to be able to let it go much faster. It doesn't seem that the magnitude of the betrayal is the determining factor. More seems to depend upon the strength of belief or faith that the betrayed has in God and His justice.

One thing seems to be common in all cases. The sooner the offended turns it over to the Lord, the sooner the relief comes. Betrayals happen in so many of the business, political, and family relationships that it seems no one is totally immune from its potentially soul-destroying impact.

The Lord's example on the cross sets the standard for all who want relief when He said: "Father, forgive them for they know not what they do" (Luke 23:34). Trying to find total relief by pursuing any other source always seems to result in less than optimal success. The one unfailing piece of advice coming from these betrayal experiences is the sooner you let God work His magic in your life, the sooner you taste the peace that comes from no other source.

POINTS TO PONDER

- Being betrayed by a trusted friend or loved one is painful. Do you harbor feelings of hatred or revenge?
- Have you tried to forgive them without their having to ask for forgiveness?
- Are you willing to allow God to be the Judge and you spend your time and energy living the life you want to live?
- Are there others you know and associate with who could benefit from your perspective on forgiving?
- Are you allowing the unrighteous acts of others to burden you and cause you to enjoy life less than you desire?

21

TURNING OUTWARD

From Selfishness to Selflessness

What good could possibly come from being isolated, locked in a hell-like prison for thirty days? This story is the account of Danny as he related it to me during and after his incarceration in the maximum-security unit of a state prison. It is condensed to meet the confines of this book.

Danny was twenty-six years old when I met him as an inmate. He was a clean-cut, handsome, well-built man with a steely look in his eyes and a smirky smile on his lips. After we became friends, he told me the following story.

I grew up in a dog-eat-dog world. I learned to fight to survive. Everything I did was to answer the question, what's in it for me? I never really stopped to consider the impact my actions had on anyone else—only if I benefitted from the activity.

It seemed that I was in trouble from my earliest age. First for shoplifting, then for petty theft. Before long, my rap sheet looked more like the introductory chapter of a book. Other than breaking car windows to steal whatever people foolishly left in plain sight, there was never anything that left people permanently hurt.

Then I started breaking into homes. I rationalized that it was unfair for some people to have so much wealth and others little or none. I felt like a modern-day Robin Hood—only I never shared what I stole with anyone else. Then came the time that a house I had cased out and was supposedly vacant at the time turned out not to be unoccupied. I don't know if the owner had a change of plans, but instead of having free reign of the house, I was met by a guy with a gun. We had a struggle, I overpowered him, and the gun went off and shot him in the stomach. He didn't die, but robbery using a weapon was no small matter.

I fled in a hurry, but before long the cops found me and hauled me off to jail. During my trial, the judge looked over my rap sheet. He shook his head in disgust and threw the book at me. That's why I ended up in central prison.

Jail is one thing; prison is something different. My fellow inmates were hardened criminals. In order not to be beat up or sodomized, I had to use my fighting skills. After one brutal fight where I sent a fellow inmate to the prison hospital, I was put in solitary confinement for a month. That was really hell. The cell was about six or seven feet wide and nine or ten feet long. It had one window about a foot square with bars every few inches. I was only permitted out for one hour a day.

Sometime during that month, I stopped plotting hurtful revenge on the guards, the inmates, and society in general. In the sullen darkness of the cell I started to reflect on the course my life was taking and what the likely outcome would be if I didn't change. It wasn't a pretty picture. I tried to analyze where I was going wrong. Like a bolt of lightning, the thought came that I needed to stop thinking of myself and start looking for ways to help others. It was such a strange idea that it took several days to think and re-think what was growing from a single thought to an almost all-consuming stream of ideas.

After lock-up I was a new man. I stopped fighting and actually tried to help some of the inmates who seemed to be struggling mentally. The day of my release the warden looked me in the eye and said, "Danny, I'll see you again before the years up!" He went on to say that the nationwide statistic indicates that more than 76 percent of the inmates would go back to prison within five years and more than 50 percent would be caught within the year. He said Central Prison had an 87 percent recidivism rate. Then he laughed and said the only reason it isn't 100 percent is that they hadn't caught the other 12 percent yet. I vowed that would never happen to me. I was determined to prove him wrong.

Freedom outside prison was more difficult than I had thought it would be. I had never had a legitimate job. Each time things got tough

I would consider going back to my life of crime. Then I would remember that time in lock-up and the decision I had made. It seemed when I had no options, a thought would come where to get a job or how to do some service to others. When I followed the thoughts, something always turned up and things worked out. Then I noticed that in addition to feeling better inside, my mind was much clearer and new opportunities came to mind. Eventually I decided to do something I thought I would never do—go back to school.

The more I considered other people, the more I was drawn to try to help them. One day I was walking by a church. It was summer and the church didn't have air conditioning so the doors were open. I sneaked in the back door and sat in one of the pews. The minister was waxing eloquent about how God knew each person and was willing to help them cope with the problems they were facing. I don't know if it was his words or the feeling that made me tingle from head to toe. At that very moment I knew what he was saying was true.

From that point in time, I tried to figure out what God wanted me to do with my life. Nothing came easy. I had many days, weeks, and months of frustration and disappointment, but through it all, I had a feeling that I couldn't turn back. I needed to keep moving forward. Eventually everything did work out. I came to know within my head and my heart that God really did know me and was leading me along.

I found a girl who could overlook my past. We got married, and things are working out better than I expected. We don't have a perfect marriage, but we both decided that we would follow God's plan that He outlined in the Bible and try to work as a team to solve our problems. It is much easier to focus on others as I try to meet my wife's needs. She is better at serving me and others than I am. But together we have noted that the more we help others, the more contentment we feel with our own lives and the surer we become that God really does know us and is helping us.

I've lost contact with Danny in the years since that interchange. But the key he mentioned about looking outside ourselves and serving others has resonated with me over the years. I have discovered the same thing in my own life—the more I serve others, the happier I am.

POINTS TO PONDER

- Life seems to demand that you watch out for yourself. Have you fallen prey to considering your own wants and needs before those of others?
- Have you ever postponed fulfilling your own needs to help someone else? How did you feel?
- Has anyone done the same for you? How did that make you feel toward them?
- Have you ever had to make a substantial sacrifice to help others?
- Have you noticed that the greater the sacrifice, the greater the feeling of reward and satisfaction that comes to you?
- Are you willing to give to the point of pain in order to help those who are in need?

22

A LIFE-CHANGING AWAKENING

From Desperation to Duty

I first met Liz at a pro-life rally. Her enthusiasm was infectious. She had a zest for what she was advocating that seemed to have no bounds. Following the rally, I sought her out and asked if she would share her story with me. She was more than willing. I wish I had recorded her story, but this is the gist of what she said:

I was a young, impressionable college student. I fashioned myself as an independent thinker as most collegians do. *Roe v. Wade* was a hot topic as the Supreme Court was deliberating the legality of abortion. Many of my social science classes evolved into fiery debates of the pros and cons advocated by both sides. Feelings often reached the boiling points as the students voiced the arguments supporting and refuting the logic presented by the media.

Somewhere along the line I determined that I was definitely pro-choice. No one should be able to tell a woman what she can and cannot do with her own body. It sounded so reasonable and logical. Little did I know that within a year I would be putting my choice to the test. Through an unwise experience at a party, and in a drunken condition where logical thinking did not rule, I became pregnant. I wasn't sure who the father would be since several had taken advantage of me that night. DNA was not fully developed in those days.

Then came the time of decision. I was single, in college, had no means of supporting a child, and was bombarded by voices advocating one side or the other. At three months I decided to end the pregnancy. I was told what the procedure entailed and that the recovery time was minimal. No one would know, and life would go on as usual. It all sounded so good. No lingering consequences from my bad experience.

The abortion was performed and everything went as predicted. That was until a few nights later when I had the first of what became regular and intensifying nightmares. A little girl with the most forlorn look on her face appeared in my nightmare. At first, she didn't say anything, but night after night she appeared, and without speaking she was able to communicate thoughts to me. She asked why I felt justified in making a decision for her that precluded her from being born and having all the experiences that other girls and women had.

At first, I could wake myself up, get a drink of water, and go back to sleep. As the nightmares continued, I found it increasingly difficult to rid the image of the little girl from my mind. Thankfully, I thought, it was only at night that I was tormented. Then the mental torment started during the waking hours. At first, I could easily dismiss the thoughts as I busied myself in schoolwork, exams, papers, and classwork. But I found that more of my days were spent wondering if I had made a terrible, irreversible mistake.

Because of the times in which we live, I decided to take a concealed weapons class at the university. During the first class the instructor made a comment that changed my thinking forever: "If you don't want the bullet to go off, don't pull the trigger. Once the trigger has been pulled, it is too late to prevent the firing of the bullet. It will discharge and it will hit whatever the gun is aimed at!"

In that moment I realized that I was both pro-choice and pro-life. If a woman doesn't want to get pregnant, then she shouldn't "pull the trigger." Of course, I realized that some pregnancies result from rape or incest, but the vast majority of unwanted pregnancies result from unprotected sex. It was like a light bulb had turned on in my mind.

I don't know if all women who have abortions experience something like I did, but I have talked with many who do. However, all the regret in the world does not restore the life I had extinguished. Was there no relief? I felt like I was being sucked into a black hole with no way out. I knew things had to change or I would lose my mind. My studies were suffering, as evidenced by my failing grades. I had no social life. My family, who lived miles away, had no idea what I was going through. I knew they would be terribly disappointed in me and possibly disown me. I felt all alone and isolated from everything and everyone. For me, the message that an abortion would "fix" everything was a big, fat lie.

At that point I felt life had ended and the only way out was to take my own life. I even went so far as to plan the time and the way of my exit. I wanted to make it look like an accident to lessen the impact on my family. My mind became obsessed with my planned escape from this virtual hell I had placed myself in.

In one of my darkest moments, I sat alone in my darkened room—blinds closed, lights out, weeping and reflecting on my life before my choice. I had grown up in a wonderful family. I loved my parents and my siblings. I had friends who acted crazy but were good kids. My life, although I had had the normal challenges all teenagers experience, was filled with sunshine and flowers, laughter and fun, dreams of a wonderful life, and hope for an eternal future with God after life was over. Was all of that gone as a vanished dream never to be reclaimed? I was pretty sure that was the gloom and doom and eternal misery that awaited me.

In desperation I cried out, "Dear God, am I lost forever?" I didn't see a vision or hear a voice, but I did feel a ray of light penetrate the suffocating darkness that engulfed me. For the first time in months, and for no logical reason since absolutely nothing had changed, I felt a sense of relief and optimism. Almost instinctively I did something I hadn't done for years—I dropped to my knees and poured out my soul to God. I told Him how sorry I was for the mistakes I had made, how I wished I could go back and live that part of life over again, how I wanted to make amends and do what I could to make things better for others, helping them avoid the same mistakes that had caused me such pain.

I didn't try to shift the blame to anyone else. I was willing to take full responsibility for my actions. I just needed to know if there was any hope for me. I wanted to know if God loved me and could ever forgive me. I wanted desperately to know if He was aware of me and would give me another chance.

I don't know how long I knelt sobbing at my bedside. It seemed like hours. But when I got up from my knees, I was a new person. In my heart of hearts, I knew that there is a God in heaven who is personally aware of me and is willing to tutor me through the challenges of life. I knew that, in time, I could be forgiven and afforded another chance to fashion, with His help, my life into something more in line with what my childhood dreams had been.

The exact course of action wasn't clearly spelled out in my mind, but the determination to find that course was unmistakable. Over the next few months, I noticed that the nightmares had ceased and the mental torment during the day no longer haunted me. I saw that people around me were friendly. I saw that many of my classmates had struggles of their own and desperately needed a kind word or a reassuring hug. Many were crying out for someone to listen to them, to talk with them, to give counsel as they struggled through their individual crisis.

Because I had lived through the hell of my own making and had watched the devastating impact it had on my life, I could easily recognize other girls who were experiencing the same soul-destroying experiences. On one such occasion I was comforting a teenager who had made the same mistake I had made, and my future role became clear: to teach others that abortion is not the best option and to offer support to women with unplanned pregnancies. Adoption, not abortion, is the answer in the vast majority of the cases I encounter. Thousands of despairing couples have tried without success to have children of their own. They would give anything to have some woman brave enough to carry her child to full-term and then allow them to adopt the child. My mission in life is to help women find the courage to help these couples.

It was like God was literally putting thoughts into my mind but so strongly punctuated with the expansive feelings of my heart. From that day on I knew the course my life was to take. Do I still have occasional recurrences of thoughts of the little girl in my nightmares? Yes, but coupled with those thoughts always comes the surge of desire to help others make wiser choices.

I don't know the plan God has concerning the destiny of the millions of children who are denied the opportunity to live their lives, but I know that He is aware of and will provide for them all. I don't expect that I will change the entire world, but I will do all in my power to influence anyone and everyone who will listen to and profit from my experience.

I walked away from that interview with a new perspective. The phrase "if you don't want the bullet to go off, don't pull the trigger" has stuck with me for many years—not only when considering the life and death decision of abortion but the virtual reality in every choice we make.

POINTS TO PONDER

- Have you made a decision that cannot be reversed?
- Has that decision impacted the course of your life?
- Can you recognize in others the signs indicating that they are going through a life-changing decision?
- How would you approach a person who is contemplating a similar mistake to the one you made?
- Would you be devastated if they refused your offer to help?
- Can you see the endless possibilities of applying the "If you don't want the bullet to go off, don't pull the trigger" principle? Could that one simple principle make a lasting impression on the way you view life?

23

HOW COULD GOD LET THIS HAPPEN TO ME?

From Frustration to Faithfulness

Unfortunately, Debbie's experience is not unique. In spite of best efforts, it still takes two to make a marriage work. Elements of this story are combined into this single scenario for the sake of brevity.

I was living the ideal life. I had married my high school sweetheart, and we had three beautiful children. We lived in a good neighborhood, and had a new home, a new car, and the debt that usually accompanies such luxury.

I was expecting our fourth child when my world came crashing down. I was completely unaware that anything was wrong in our marriage or family life. So, when my husband informed me that he had had enough and was abandoning me and the children, I was left speechless.

What had I done wrong? Was I no longer physically appealing—especially in my pregnant condition? Were there warning flags that I missed? To my pleadings for understanding, I received no satisfactory answers. Just like that twelve years of marriage were shattered. He took the car but left me the monthly payment. I had been a stay-at-home mom, and since we had married before I finished college, I had no degree to use as a credential for good employment. My fourth child was due to be born in two months. There seemed to be no plausible answers to the endless questions the children were asking about their daddy. I felt totally abandoned—which I was!

Sobbing alone in my bedroom after the children were in bed did nothing but exacerbate the hopeless condition I found myself in. How was I to provide for my family? Would we have to move to an apartment? How could I buy another car with no income? What would happen when the baby was born? How could I pay the hospital and doctor bills? Endless questions plagued my mind with no obvious answers.

One night in total desperation I fell to my knees and pleaded with God for some help. I think I remember waking up still kneeling alongside my bed. I thought God must be disgusted with me—falling asleep while talking with Him. However, early the next morning a knock came at the door. Looking like I hadn't slept all night—which I really hadn't—I opened the door to find my next-door neighbor standing with a bag of groceries. She invited herself in and explained that she had heard what happened and had watched as my husband had driven away a few days earlier and had never returned. She said the neighbors had huddled to find ways of helping me adjust. I was blown away. It was like God had heard my muddled prayer and was working behind the scenes to help meet my immediate needs.

Over the course of the next few days, I learned that one of the neighbors had an old car he was willing to donate so I would have transportation. Another neighbor had a business that would allow me to work from home so I could be a mom and a breadwinner. Several other neighbors offered to tend my children when I needed some time alone or to go grocery shopping. A neighbor I hardly knew was a doctor. He said he had made arrangements to have the baby delivered at the hospital where he worked and that the hospital administrator had agreed to defer payment until I could earn the money to pay the costs.

Along the way I had developed the practice of daily prayer, morning and night, with the children and many times alone during the day. As I became more dependent upon God for the mental and physical strength to carry on, I began to realize that He was definitely answering my prayers. I had sufficient energy to meet the demands of the children, do the house work, and fulfill my job at home. Often there wasn't much energy left over at the end of the day. When I felt I was mentally going under and needed a break, without asking a neighbor would show up and offer to babysit while

I had some time alone. It seemed that these "coincidences" were like little miracles that came at just the right time.

The baby's birth was met with the same timely miracles. It just so happened that when I went into labor while two neighbors were visiting. One drove me to the hospital while the other watched the children, fed them, and put them to bed. The delivery went well, and the recovery was faster than the other three had been. Soon I was at home enjoying a new little daughter, and the other children were thrilled beyond words to hold and cuddle the new arrival.

Time marched on. There were tough times, sad times, happy times, frustrating time—all one normally experiences in life. My husband never contacted me again, never offered any financial support, and never tried to be part of the lives of his children.

It has been almost six years since my life collapsed around me. While at a neighborhood picnic last week, a friend of a neighbor, a widower, struck up a conversation with me. He said he was interested in seeing me again. I'm not sure if anything will come of this relationship, but it was a shot to my ego that I was still appealing enough for a man to want to associate with me knowing that I had four children to support.

In trying to sort through all the ups and downs of the past six years, I have come to know beyond a doubt that there is a God in heaven who knows me and is there to help me through the good times as well as the tough times. I can see growth in myself that I hadn't ever seen before. I discovered talents I hadn't expanded, personality traits I didn't know I had, and people skills that drew others to me. Yes, life has evolved in a way I didn't anticipate and didn't want. But I know for sure that whatever may come next, with the unwavering help of God and the support of neighbors and friends, I can not only survive but actually thrive. Some may say that what I call "little miracles" are just coincidental happenings. I know for myself that God really is involved in my life, and I give Him praise multiple times each day.

It has taken a long time to forgive my husband for abandoning me and the children. There was so much anger at first. Then I discovered that my hatred for him was only stifling my spiritual growth. I believe in a God who is fair and just. He will balance the scales of eternal justice. I don't have to worry about that. Now, after six years, I have more pity for him than hatred. I see what he is missing as I watch the children grow and change. I now hope (and this has been a long time in coming) that he finds happiness in his new life. Someday I'll understand more fully why a loving God allowed such a trial to come to me and my family. For now I am content to know that I don't have to meet the challenges alone. If God is with you, you are never alone.

Many times, the challenging trials we face are not the result of our own actions but the unrighteous decisions of others. Asking "why me?" is usually not productive. Being aware of the mini-miracles and being willing to ask God for help often point one in the right direction, resulting in personal growth and happiness in spite of the setback.

POINTS TO PONDER

- People all around you are silently crying out for help because of conditions they do not deserve and do not want. Are you tuned in to the needs of those around you? How do you recognize those people?
- Would you be willing to put yourself out in organizing help for such a person?
- Has anyone ever noticed a need in your life and without asking came to your assistance?
- How did you feel about them? Are there people right now, today, who need your help?
- Are you willing to leave your comfort zone and help them?

24

A DRINK THAT DESTROYS

From Recklessness to Resolve

Unfortunately, this chapter comes too close to home for me. My father became an alcoholic after suffering an injury at the end of World War II that rendered him paraplegic. His drinking and other problems resulted in an early death at the age of thirty-three, leaving my mother to raise five children ages eleven through three. Partly because of my father's early death (I was four and a half years old at the time), I became a people watcher. From a very early age I have tried to figure out why some people are successful and happy, while others seem to pursue happiness in ways that result in misery and heartache to themselves and everyone they associate with. Such is the story of two brothers, Darrel and Devon, both lifelong alcoholics. Darrel tells their story.

Devon and I have always been the best of friends as well as brothers. What one did, the other was not far behind. Our father worked away from home much of the time. When he was home, he was usually drunk. Mom raised the family. It was somewhere in our early teen years that we discovered a bottle of our father's liquor. We sneaked it out to the barn and each drank half the bottle. It didn't taste good and made us both sick to our stomachs. However, we rationalized that we must have gotten a bad bottle or Dad wouldn't drink so much.

A second sneaked bottle made us both drunk but not sick. From there it was a downhill slide. We left home as soon as we could and got an apartment in the city. We each had a good job that paid well, but most of our money, beyond rent and utilities, went toward booze.

We actually ended up marrying sisters. Although neither of them drank, they voiced their concern about our drinking, but we continued. We rationalized that we could quit any time we wanted to. Each of our wives had to get a job to support our growing families because most of our money went to booze.

We recognized that our children, as they got older, were embarrassed to invite their friends to our houses, which were across the street from each other. We had been drinking for so many years that we were sure we could "hold our liquor" and no one would recognize that we were drunk. We didn't have many friends, but we had each other.

Our children grew up and moved away. Surprisingly, our wives stayed with us. In retrospect, they should have bailed long before. Life as we knew it was good. Until Devon started to get sick. We got him to the doctor, who said if he didn't stop drinking, his body would start shutting down and he'd die. That scared both of us and we decided to stop drinking.

It didn't turn out that way. Trying to support each other, we would get depressed and felt the only way of coping was to take another little drink. We promised each other that we would only have one little drink. That was a lie. We knew one drink would just open the floodgates and we'd be back at it again.

Devon's health continued to deteriorate. I was doing fine. The day before Devon died, he called me to his bedside and made me promise to straighten up my life and make something more of myself than he had made of his life. His death was a serious wake-up call for me. I comforted his widow and promised to help take care of her. She gave me that look as if to say, "We have been taking care of you two all of our married lives. Why should I expect any help from you now?" It was like a knife to my heart.

I did something I hadn't done for years. After the funeral I drove to the nearby canyon and got down on my knees and prayed to God for the strength to straighten up my life. I don't remember any miraculous feeling or experience but just a firm resolve to make it happen this time.

Without Devon to drink with, and with a resolve to straighten up, I started praying regularly. I was too ashamed to pray with my wife for fear she would think I was being a total hypocrite. I secretly starting reading the Bible. I can't put my finger on the exact time or place that I felt an inner strength come to me that I had never felt before. It felt like Devon was helping me from the spirit world. Somehow, I knew that God was there cheering me on and offering to help when I would get discouraged and depressed.

I got a job, cleaned up the way I looked, and started trying to be pleasant around my formerly abused wife. It wasn't too long when both she and Devon's wife noticed the difference in me. They asked me what was going on. I told them I was making good my promise to Devon to make something of myself.

I wish I could say the transformation was immediate. It wasn't. My longing for alcohol was occasionally so strong that only pleading prayer saved me from relapsing. I knew for sure I had to stay away from my old drinking buddies and avoid the places where alcohol is served. Eventually I learned how to control my attitude and behavior to be more acceptable to my wife and sister-in-law. Often, I turned to God in prayer, pleading for some inspiration on how to overcome some undesirable trait or habit. It seemed the Lord was always there. I came to know that He knew me and was vitally interested in my success.

I only wish Devon and I had never sneaked the first bottle of booze. I wish my father had realized the impact his drinking had on us. I am not blaming him or anyone but ourselves. We should have known better. I really wish we had turned to God when the doctor told Devon that continuing to drink would shorten his life. I wish Devon could have experienced the happiness and joy I feel now that I'm free from the drink that destroys lives.

Many positive things resulted from the drinking death of my father. One major blessing is that I have never tasted alcohol. I don't know if I have a genetic predisposition that would lead me to an easy addiction. I don't have to worry as long as I never take the first drink.

For those who are struggling to free themselves from the tentacles of alcohol or drug addiction, like so many before, I certify that there is hope and there is a way out. It may not be easy or painless, but with the help of a loving, caring, personal God, all things are possible.

POINTS TO PONDER

- Have you considered that a person with an addiction is as much in prison as one who is physically incarcerated?
- Are you free from agency-destroying habits?
- Have you considered the impact your attitude and behavior have on your spouse and family and your friends?
- Are there areas where you would do well to consider and change?
- Are you humble enough to ask those around you for help in overcoming your habit?
- Have you considered helping others who are struggling but want to change?
- Can you help others without passing judgment on them?

25

FAITH OF OUR FATHERS ABANDONED

From Trials to Tenacity

Shawn's story has caused me more deep reflection than almost any other. I wish I had the ability to tell it with the clarity and spirit that he recounted it to me. Shawn is a lifelong friend. We grew up together in the same neighborhood. We certainly were not perfect kids, but we were good kids nonetheless. Shawn said:

As you know, I grew up in a great family. Our common saying was "we have everything that money can't buy." We were happy, had a close group of friends, and enjoyed life to the max. We would skinny drip in the local river, play football almost every summer evening, tease the girls, play night games, and participate in town clean-up projects.

I attended church every Sunday because my family did and all my friends were there. It wasn't until my later teen years that I began to question my beliefs. I kept up the appearance of being fully engaged in order to avoid the interrogation and pressure I knew would follow if I revealed how I really felt. It wasn't too difficult to sneak out to smoke a few cigarettes and drink a few beers. When questioned about the odor of tobacco and beer, it was easy to explain that several in the group were messing around, but I lied to hide that I was participating.

Graduation from high school and going off to college afforded me the opportunity to flex my muscles and spread my wings. No one was there to monitor my behavior. I was free—or so I thought. I was still pretty "straight" according to the standards of my newfound college friends, but I did engage in more parties than before. I remember the night my friends talked me into smoking a joint of marijuana for the first time. I felt free from the drudgery of life. Life was good.

After my initial experience with drugs, it was not long before I convinced myself that it was just innocent fun and that I could stop anytime I wanted to. It was such a gradual decline that I found myself buying into the lie that I was in complete control. I discovered, however, that after some time, what was thrilling and satisfying in both drinking and drugs fails to give the same satisfaction as it previously had. I had to drink more, do more and stronger drugs, and push the limits with activities my friends were engaged in to achieve the same pseudo-high that I had enjoyed before.

In retrospect, it was a regrettable night when immorality was added to the activities of that party. Under the influence of alcohol, with my mind clouded and my resistance down and the girl a willing participant, I gave up what I had always promised myself would be saved for my future wife. But, in all honesty, it was thrilling. It wasn't until the next morning, suffering from a terrible hangover, that I sensed the regret that would become my near-constant companion. In order to mask the pain, I started drinking more, doing more and harder drugs, and sleeping around more often. There was always the ultimate lie that true happiness lay just around the next corner. The next high would be the one that would satisfy. The next sexual encounter would be the ultimate euphoric expression of true love. None of that proved to be true.

I found who I thought was the girl of my dreams my last year in college. She was near perfect—a true church-goer and a principled individual, in addition to her unparalleled beauty and superior intellect. I felt like I had really been heaven blessed. We were married and started a life together. It wasn't until after the honeymoon that she discovered the depth of my addictions. Patiently she said we would work through the addictions and regain my freedom.

Her efforts brought remarkable results. I was basically clean with very few relapses with drugs or alcohol. I had committed to be faithful to her sexually. I can't begin to express how happy I was as she announced the forthcoming birth of our first child. Life couldn't have been better. I graduated college and got a good job. We purchased a modest house, and with the birth of our son everything seemed to be on course for a happy, fulfilling life.

One day I ran into an old friend—one of my drinking buddies. He invited me to grab a bite to eat and catch up. With the idea in mind of pulling him away from drugs and alcohol, I agreed. Unfortunately, as you can suspect, just the opposite happened. He enticed me to have just one beer—for old time's sake. I reluctantly gave in.

Then the lying began. When queried by my wife I told her about the meal but lied about the smell of beer as being from my friend. Over the course of years, I continued to sneak out and have a beer and do a few drugs. Two more children were born—a little girl and another boy. Then came the fatal night when I went to a party with my friends while my wife's mother was home helping her with our newborn son. I hadn't been intimate with my wife for some time due to the closeness of her delivery. There was an old friend at the party who had been intimate with me before I straightened up. She reminded me of the "good old days" and enticed me for a quick tussle for "old time's sake." I gave in. I couldn't bring myself to confess to my wife. I knew it would weaken our marriage and destroy her confidence in me.

The cheating scenario was reenacted many more times. Then came the day a friend told my wife what she had observed. My wife confronted me, and I reluctantly confessed. She said she was willing to work it out and stay with me on the condition that it never happened again. I humbly accepted the condition. However, before long, I broke my promise and it broke my marriage.

The divorce was extremely painful. I really loved my wife and adored my children. Now all of that was taken away. I can't blame my wife for not sticking with such a loser. I knew she deserved much better. I got an apartment and moved out. At first, I was diligent in providing alimony and child support. But over time the escalating costs of drugs and alcohol caused me to rationalize that I couldn't afford those monthly family support expenses. Soon the law was after me threatening to garnish my wages to meet my family obligations.

On top of all those problems, my efficiency at work diminished, my appearance deteriorated, and before long I was terminated from my job. Now with no legal means of supporting myself, my addictions, and my family, I began to sell drugs. I was evicted from my apartment and literally became homeless. If you look at so many homeless people, you will see what I looked like—unshaven, unbathed, filthy clothes, and a continual downcast look.

I learned from others that my wife had remarried a good man and seemed very happy as she moved on with her life. My children didn't even remember me. I was lost and alone. The slippery slope of addiction had taken me to the edge of the cliff. I knew I couldn't go on. Suicide looked like the only acceptable option to end the constant pain. My mind was so darkened that it was difficult to follow a logical train of thought. I felt like I was caught in a filthy pool of quicksand and couldn't get out. Once I was considered by others to be near genius. Now it felt more like I had a single-digit IQ.

I was afraid to take my life because I had known that there is an afterlife, and I knew I would not have a welcome reception there. In the absolute depths of despair, head in hands, I cried out to God to just make me disappear. I didn't want to live forever, and I knew that living in a place described as eternal fire and brimstone held no appeal.

It was at that crisis junction when I felt abandoned and totally alone that I bumped into an old friend from our teenage years. He didn't recognize me, but I recognized him. I wanted to hide from him, but something compelled me to approach him. At first, he thought I was just another bum wanting a handout to support a habit. Then there was a glimmer of recognition. When he recognized me, he puts his arms around me and pulled me into the first warm, meaningful embrace that I had had in years. I wept on his shoulder. He took me to a nearby restaurant and bought me the first hot meal I had enjoyed in a very long time. We talked about the good old days. I learned that he was a happily married dentist with five children and a loving wife. Then, to my utter surprise and amazement, he offered to help me clean up my life.

He asked me to remember the happiest times of my life. Of course, I recounted our youth, then my marriage and children. I told him my wife had remarried and moved on and my children didn't even remember me as their father. He told me what I already knew—those times with the wife and children were gone and could not be reclaimed. But then he said with the help of God I could build a new life and avoid making the mistakes that had destroyed my old life. I really needed to hear those words. He reminded me that God is literally the Father of our spirits and that He is very interested in our well-being and is willing to be as involved in our lives as we permit Him to be. This was the first time someone had given me hope that all was not lost, that I could, with the help of God, return—like the prodigal son in the New Testament—and be greeted by a loving, caring Heavenly Father.

It almost sounded like it was too good to be true, but there was a feeling inside that whispered, "What he is saying is true." I knew it wouldn't be easy and that I would likely relapse many times, but at last I had hope that I could make it. I readily admit that it wasn't a cake walk. It was the toughest thing I have ever done—going through multiple rehabs, being shunned by good people who have little patience with those who are struggling, falling and getting up again and again and again. Finally I saw progress and felt the light return in my life.

It was a happy day when I landed a good job and was able to rent an apartment and buy my own food and clothes. It was even a happier day when I started dating a woman who saw in me what I did not see in myself. It has not been easy, but we got married and have started a life together based on the principles that I turned my back on in church years ago.

What is the key? Never give up on yourself. As soon as you turn toward God and the Light, He will give you the help you need to pick yourself up, dust yourself off, and give it another go. Some opportunities are gone and cannot be reclaimed. Some experiences lost cannot be reenacted. But that doesn't mean that there aren't opportunities and experiences yet ahead that can enrich your life. Someday I hope to be able to apologize to my former wife and children. For right now, I have my hands full trying to build a new home, a new marriage, a new career, and a new life.

Shawn and I keep in touch with each other. The ensuing years have brought joy and happiness to him and his new family that he didn't think possible. He has also become a source of help to others who have made the same mistakes and feel they are lost forever. He is a strong advocate of holding fast to the faith of our fathers, developing a closer relationship with God, and being constantly aware of the promptings that come from heaven to each of us as we encounter the challenges of life.

POINTS TO PONDER

- It is far too easy to look at one who has bottomed out and say they deserve to be where they are. It is much more benevolent to take a person where they are and try to help them. Are you willing to help the helpless and downtrodden?
- How far will you go in your attempts to help?
- Has anyone helped you when you were having a tough time? How did you feel toward them?
- When doors are closed because of transgression, are you willing to forgive yourself and start over?
- Can you identify what mistakes you made along the way and avoid making them again?

26

IF NOT GOD, THEN WHAT?

A Serious Look Inward

When it comes right down to the bottom line, without trying to make the decision too simple, the question every thinking, reasoning person must ask is, does God exist or did this whole environment around us happen by chance? It is obvious from the vignettes in this book that I am a devout believer in God. However, I respect the right of every person to come to his or her own conclusion.

If you have never had that soul-searching debate with yourself, a few ideas may act as a catalyst to get the debate going. In considering the possibility of everything from the macrocosmic universes to the microscopic sub-atoms, the question comes to my mind, when did the whole thing start? Even if I mentally chase back through the endless generations of creation, I cannot come to an answer about the very first "big bang" or whatever scientists choose to call it.

While it is true that I cannot envision a time or how the "First Cause" came into being, it is much more plausible in my mind that some super intelligence crafted what exists around us today. If we only consider this earth and the diversity of life we see around us, it is beyond my ability to comprehend how people can believe that all of this came about by a chance meeting of some primordial material and then evolved over countless ages into the diversity we see around us. The statistical probability of that happening goes far beyond anything a reasoning person can visualize. Yet the scientific world goes to great lengths to "prove" or at least appear to prove, that is the explanation of how life began. All of that seems to be with one purpose: Find an explanation of how things are that does not include God.

On the other hand, those who have a faith in a Higher Power, no matter what form it takes, find a plausible explanation in the first verse in the Bible, which states, "In the beginning God created the heaven and the earth" (Genesis 1:1). Now, whether we choose to believe in God or in evolution, it seems wise to consider the ramifications of our decision.

If we are merely an extension of an endless evolutionary process, then there really is no right or wrong, only as mankind can agree. If, on the other hand, God really did create man after His own image and revealed a plan to enable mankind to return to His presence, then right becomes something God states is right and wrong is defined by what God says is wrong. Part of the conflict that seems to endlessly swirl around us is the fact that a growing portion of humankind has embraced the evolutionary philosophy. That doesn't suggest that there are no morals in the world, rather that there are no absolutes when analyzing right and wrong.

If the evolutionary theory is correct, then there is no real purpose in earth life. Only eat, drink, and be merry and live until you die. If there is no postmortal life, then life should be prolonged as long as possible and death avoided at any cost. On the other hand, if one believes in God, then following what He has revealed in scriptures, there is a definite purpose for mortal life: to prepare to reunite with God at the conclusion of mortal life. Death becomes more like a graduation from the difficulties of mortal life to a life without pain, suffering, and disease.

While there are many people who do not profess a belief in God who are good neighbors, compassionate individuals, and helpful members of society, those qualities all exist on a "by choice" basis and not by divine design. If a person chooses to abandon acceptable moral behavior, he is allowed to do so as long as his chosen behavior does not infringe on the rights of other people. If he chooses to go beyond what society accepts as normal, there are prisons and possible execution awaiting him.

To one who does not believe in God, one's worth is determined by societal rules. If one believes in God, one's goodness is measured against one's adherence to the commandments of God.

If there is no purpose in life other than surviving day to day, then pleasure and indulgence have a greater appeal. However, if there is purpose in life which embraces the philosophy of preparing for the next life, restraint, controlled behavior, and consideration of the impact one's behavior has on others in society becomes very important.

When challenges in life confront one who denies the existence of God, the likely outcome is anger and frustration. On the other hand, if one believes in God when those same challenges come, they are faced with some belief that there is merit in the challenge and seen as an opportunity for growth rather than a happiness-destroying distraction from our pursuit of pleasure without pain.

Mere belief in God is not sufficient to give meaning to life. An agnostic may profess to believe in God but does not believe that He is involved in one's life. Such an approach supposedly "frees" the person from the necessity of conforming his or her life to a set of revealed standards. Therefore, the promised blessing for obedience are never realized. From my perspective, an agnostic, in attempting to take the neutral position in the argument for or against God, does himself the greatest of all disservices. In times of stress or crisis, he may turn to God expecting that, if there is a God, perhaps He will break His isolationism and this one time intercede on his behalf. Even if God does intervene and help the struggling agnostic, as soon as the crisis is over, the agnostic likely will revert to his former mental state, thus achieving no noticeable growth or refinement.

I have often wondered what the reaction of an atheist would be when he dies and finds that there is a life after death. At that point will he be willing to admit his mistake? Or will he be like the ancient Israelites who refused to look at the brazen serpent on Moses' pole and died a painful death when the antidote was readily available? (see Numbers 21:6–9).

What of these scientific seekers after truth? Because God cannot be quantified and confined to a laboratory test tube for analysis, does that really indicate that He does not exist? When the Lord gave a surefire way of determining whether what He said was true, are they really sincere when they refuse to follow this simple test: "If any man will do his will, he shall know of the doctrine, whether it be of God, or whether I speak of myself" (John 7:17).

So, if not God, then what? Not taking the time to ask that question may be robbing you of the close association the Savior promised when He said, "Ask, and it shall be given you; seek, and ye shall find; knock, and it shall be opened unto you: For **every one that asketh receiveth**; and he that seeketh findeth; and to him that knocketh it shall be opened" (Matthew 7:7–8, emphasis added). Sounds like an open invitation and challenge to me. Rather than risk one more day of living without God in your life, why not put God to the test and receive the promised reward?

POINTS TO PONDER

- People generally exchange what they have for something better. If you have considered turning your back on God, what are you hoping in exchange that is better?
- Have you talked with others who have lost their faith in God?
- How is their level of enjoyment in life?
- If they are having a good time, have they considered what is at the end of their life?
- Are you serious in considering what happens after death? Have you given God a fair try by keeping His commandments and looking for the promised rewards?

EPILOGUE

Each of the vignettes in this book has pointed to the fact that people have found themselves when they have turned to the Light. Some evidence of divine involvement happened immediately; other transformations took time. Every one of them immediately experienced that spark of enlightenment that generated hope and gave them the courage and determination to continue their quest. If you have read the entire book, you have likely had thoughts of scenarios you could have added. In summary, and as a transition to what is available going forward, I would refer you to the following principles found in the Bible.

Paul, an ancient Apostle, after a long and difficult road from persecutor of Christians, to being persecuted by his former friends, to becoming a powerful advocate for that which he had come to understand, wrote the following: "I can do all things through Christ which strengtheneth me" (Philippians 4:13). Where did he get that confidence? Through his own experience and watching the impact that Christ had in the lives of all those who accepted Him.

When the Angel Gabriel was explaining to Mary how she would become the mother of the Son of God since she was not married, he said: "For with God nothing shall be impossible" (Luke 1:37). What appears to man to be impossible is certainly within the scope of God's unlimited power.

Now compare those two very bold statements with what the Lord said about man's abilities using only his own power: "I am the vine, ye are the branches: He that abideth in me, and I in him, the same bringeth forth much fruit: **for without me ye can do nothing**" (John 15:5, emphasis added).

In my mind's eye I see a non-believer entering a darkened room. Instinctively he reaches for the electrical switch to turn on the lights. He flips the switch and the room is immediately illuminated. Smugly, he thinks within himself that he created the light. He seems unaware that behind the switch are electrical lines leading to the breaker panel in his home. From there the lines are connected to the power lines on the street. The lines then travel through transformers, increasing the power to a grid system that distributes the electricity. From there larger and more powerful lines follow back to some generating source—it might be water generated, solar, nuclear, coal, natural gas, or any other source. Without all of those elements in place, flipping the switch would be a fruitless effort.

Accepting or denying that the intricate system described above exists has absolutely nothing to do with the reality. Understanding or accepting that God exists and is working behind the scenes has no effect on the fact that He is there and as the Lord said, "Without Him we can do nothing!" We wouldn't even exit.

Arrogant man has come to believe that he and he alone, independent of any outside influences, can accomplish anything he sets his mind to. What an eye-opening experience awaits all of us when we pass from earth life to the next life to see how intimately God has been involved in virtually everything we have been able to accomplish.

Consider this teaching the Lord gave to His followers: "Are not five sparrows sold for two farthings, and not one of them is forgotten before God? But even the very hairs of your head are all numbered. Fear not therefore: ye are of more value than many sparrows" (Luke 12:6–7).

Connecting all of these thoughts: With God all things are possible that He wills to happen. Even if those things are impossible to man—such as parting the Red Sea to allow liberated Israel to cross on dry grounds (and countless other examples portrayed in the Bible)—linking up with Christ, we can do anything as long as it is consistent with God's will. Miracles never will cease as long as men and women acknowledge God's involvement in their lives and seek to know His will. Even though we may not be aware of divine involvement in our lives (like the flipping of an electrical switch to turn on the lights), God is *always* there and is involved in the happenings of our lives to the most minute detail (like numbering the very hairs of our heads).

Whether or not we accept that analogy has absolutely no effect on whether it exists. How much better would the person flipping the electrical switch be if he recognized all of the superstructure behind the power, and then explored the endless ways that power could be used to enrich his own life and the lives of all around him?

This book has been written to help people awake to the fact that God is involved in their lives. Now, if you have accepted that, possibly the next step would be to look more carefully at the word of God and see if He has organized laws or outlined requirements for achieving desired blessings. Taking that as a challenge, for many years I have tried to quantify the requirements for receiving certain blessings. Everything around us suggests that God is a God of law. When we obey the law, we are blessed. When we, knowingly or unknowingly, break the law, we suffer the consequences. Consider gravity, for example. It doesn't make any difference if we believe in it or deny its existence. If we step off a tall building, we inescapably suffer the consequences unless we take steps to counteract the fall—such as deploying a parachute.

With that idea in mind, I have searched the scriptures for many years and have written another book intended to be a sequel to this book. The title has yet to be finalized. I suspect you would find it an exciting and eye-opening book. As with the scenarios in this book, as you read my other book, you will see more blessings you would like to enjoy, and then, as you search the scriptures, you will discover where the Lord has outlined the requirements for achieving those blessings.

One thing is undeniable: as you turn your focus toward God, your whole perspective on life will change. If you are already God-focused, you will experience an unquestionable increase in your enjoyment of life and your understanding of the trials that inescapably follow. This earth life was not meant to be a cakewalk. The Lord said, "These things I have spoken unto you, that in me ye might have peace. In the world ye shall have tribulation: but be of good cheer; I have overcome the world" (John 16:33).

The choice is yours! Look to God and expand your vision, your enjoyment, and your desire to draw close to Him, or continue in the course you may have been pursuing for a lifetime and receive the same level of enjoyment you have experienced to this point. What do you have to lose by turning toward the Light?

ABOUT THE AUTHOR

Randy Bott is married to the love of his life, Vickie (fifty years and counting). They have six children, sixteen grandchildren, and one great-granddaughter.

Brother Bott has degrees from Utah State University (a bachelor's in psychology and a master's in secondary education) and a doctorate degree in educational leadership from Brigham Young University. He has served as a bishop, in two stake presidencies, and as a mission president. He served his first mission in Samoa.

After he retired from BYU in 2012, he and his wife served missions at BYU–Hawaii and in Sydney, Australia. They are currently preparing for another mission.

Brother Bott taught in the Church Education System in Utah and North Carolina for twenty years, and nineteen years at BYU–Provo. He has authored many books and articles. His passion is teaching and counseling. He loves people and loves problem-solving and creating new programs to help people succeed.

NOTES

NOTES

NOTES